The First Year

The First Year

A Retirement Journal by John Mosedale

Crown Publishers, Inc.
New York

Published by Crown Publishers, Inc., 201 East 50th Street, New York, New York 10022. Member of the Crown Publishing Group.

Random House, Inc. New York, Toronto, London, Sydney, Auckland

CROWN is a trademark of Crown Publishers, Inc.

Manufactured in the United States of America
Book Design by Mercedes Everett

Library of Congress Cataloging-in-Publication Data
Mosedale, John.
      The first year : a retirement journal / by John Mosedale. — 1st ed.
        p.   cm.
      1. Mosedale, John.   2. Journalists—United States—Biography.
      3. Television broadcasting of news—United States.   4. Retirement—
United States.   I. Title.
    PN4874.M588A3   1993
    070'.92—dc20
      [B]   92–31658
                                                                            CIP

ISBN 0–517–58641–X

10   9   8   7   6   5   4   3   2   1

First Edition

For Molly

❖ ❖ ❖ ❖ ❖

Betty is my wife. Amy, Laura, Andrew, and Michael are our children, who are adults. Matt is Laura's husband. All of them, when this journal began, lived in New York City, except for Michael, who was working as a newspaperman in Superior, Wisconsin.

Betty's mother, called Yia Yia by our children, was in a nursing home in Maryland. Betty's father died in 1971.

My mother died in 1961. My sister Dote died in 1971. My sister Anne died in 1986.

All are part of what follows.

❖ ❖ ❖ ❖ ❖

The First Year

Walking Away from It
Friday, February 1, 1991

Today is the first day of my retirement.

On my desk, amid a dispiriting landfill of books, papers, newspaper and magazine articles, and theater and opera playbills, is a letter from CBS Business Affairs, dated January 21.

"Dear John," it reads, "This letter confirms our conversation whereby you advised me that you will be retiring on February 1, 1991, and that January 31, 1991, will be the last day of your employment with us. I have attached hereto . . . "

That communication marked the official end of almost thirty years at CBS television for me, a gaudy time when I wrote news for Walter Cronkite and Dan Rather, for Harry Reasoner and Charles Kuralt and Douglas Edwards, and, while nations and airplanes and the economy crashed, I wrote sports for Jack Whitaker and Brent Musburger and Phyllis George and Tom Harmon and Jimmy the Greek, swinging back and forth from news to sports to news, swinging.

I suspect anyone who retires asks where the time went. For me, it went in a seamless blur of events—how vital! how quickly forgotten!—events that qualified as news by my judgment or by the judgment of my colleagues. I wrote at ten national political conventions, two Super Bowls, three space shots, one of which nearly killed me. I wrote about the deaths of presidents and movie stars and rock stars, violence in the streets, Vietnam and drugs and corporate malefactors. I attended the Royal Wedding for CBS, and a motor car safari in Kenya.

There were three writers and an editor when I wrote for the evening news: a foreign writer, a national writer, who chiefly wrote about Washington, and the writer called "all else." I was "all else." I said my job was to write about the economy and other natural disasters. Let the government issue an unemployment report, let a train derail, let a picture of the Virgin appear mysteriously on a corn silo, and I was set to reduce the event to a couple of lines, which is ten or fifteen seconds of the anchor's time.

I loved my work. I also found it humbling. Writing is hard and writing under deadline is harder. We kidded a lot, but all the writers I worked with tried for fairness. Most of the time that I wrote for Walter and later for Dan "The CBS Evening News" was the top-rated evening news broadcast. We routinely addressed an audience of millions. On a slow news day in August, we reached more people than the best-selling book or the largest-circulation newspaper. We took the responsibility of informing people seriously. We were regularly denounced from the White House, the pulpit, the street. What we did was important. People, millions of them, who didn't know our names paid attention to what we wrote.

I left all that last night.

Even though it is the work we do that identifies us—we are a doctor, a businessman, a teacher; we don't refer to "my friend Frank, the husband," we say, "My friend Frank, the plumber"—the more important part of my life is anonymous. While the world convulsed and calmed, Betty and I raised four children. We made enduring friendships, and friendships that dissolved in busyness. We went to the theater and movies and parties, too many parties for me, for a while, and we shared decades of laughter and some sorrow, deaths in the family and among friends.

Family and friends are the part of life you do not retire from.

When I walked out of CBS Studio 47 for the last time as a worker there, I headed into a future that no longer defined itself in a newsroom. In retirement, I am on my own, to make a new life, not a living. I told myself, I tell myself, I have a wife and children to cherish, writing to do, libraries to read, plays and operas and football games to gape at.

And yet, and yet, there remains that great space which I filled by writing news. Pascal said, "The silence of these infinite spaces terrifies me." On a more worldly level, I think that is what the idea of retirement means—a sudden silence after the roar of work.

People asked me what it was like to write for Walter or Dan. I said I spent the day in laughter that ended in panic. The hard part of the day on the evening news always came at the end of the day. "6:29:30," the hour in New York when we went on the air, was a newsroom trope for terror and despair.

There is never enough time in the newsroom. The terrible hand of the clock always advances the deadline. A producer once challenged me, "Name another business where at five o'clock in the afternoon on Friday you wished it were earlier."

Now trickster time poses a different challenge.

I recently received a letter from a retired businessman who said he thought he would go crazy if it weren't for his once-a-week volunteer work. I am afraid I will go crazy if that is all that keeps me from going crazy.

I have charms in my pocket, toys up my sleeve. I have Betty. I have the children. I have Shakespeare and operas and trying to learn Italian. The question is: will the charms work?

I decided years ago that when I reached sixty-five, I would quit whatever I was doing and do something else. Disbelieving colleagues said, "What are you going to do when you retire?" I said, "I will sit around the apartment and watch Betty."

The people I worked with kept getting younger. It had occurred to me that if "The CBS Evening News" were a war movie, I would be the man called "Pops." We all know what happens in war movies to the man called "Pops."

What will I do away from the laughter and the curses, the dry throat and the wet palms of writing copy while we are on the air, the fights over a ten-second haiku meant to explain unemployment, suffering the bends over a story no one will remember tomorrow? What does the lawyer do without clients, the businessman without an invoice, the clerk without a ribbon?

I will keep this journal to see what happens during the first year of my retirement, what will fill the days and nights without the daily adrenaline shot of the deadline.

This will be a journal, not a diary. I think that in a journal, the writer shapes his experience into something like essays. He stands back and considers. He reveals only what is important to his purpose. *Walden* is a journal, as is *One Man's Meat*. H. L. Mencken's diaries are diaries, and people who read them got what they deserved. No honest person keeps a diary with an eye to publication for at least a century. Our selves are too dark.

I expect to face the same emotional and psychological problems faced by the businesswoman who retires, the punch press operator, or the policeman. Like the computer scientist, certain medical specialists, or a rock musician, I am retiring from a line of work that didn't exist when I was a child.

The place I walked away from changed the way people thought and perceived.

When I was a boy in Milwaukee in the 1930s, television was a fantasy, as remote as space travel. I learned about television not in the pages of *Popular Science* but in *The Ring* magazine, "Boxing's Bible," which carried an account of a fight in England that was transmitted to a movie theater by something called television.

About that time, in 1938, E. B. White took leave of *The New Yorker* to settle on a farm in Maine. He ploughed, producing an imperishable harvest in the form of a column called "One Man's Meat" for *Harper's* magazine.

The world was coming to an end in 1938. Radio was what television became, a ubiquitous presence. Radio's voice followed White around the farm. He also read newspapers, including news of the fiction called "television."

White looked into the future and wondered if it would work.

"I believe that television is going to be the test of the modern world," he wrote, "and that in this new opportunity to see beyond the range of our vision, we shall discover either a new and unbearable disturbance of the general peace or a saving radiance in the sky. We shall stand or fall by television—of that I am quite sure."

As I walked away last night, I saw no saving radiance in the sky above the Broadcast Center there in Hell's Kitchen. Almost everyone seems to watch television, however, and almost everyone seems to watch it more than Betty and I do. I watch news and football. Betty watches news. We watch "Sunday Morning." The last series we watched regularly was "The Mary Tyler Moore Show," when our children were little. I think television was more fun to write for than to watch.

I used to tell the children that what I did at CBS was God's work. I was only half kidding. I saw a news god presiding over our activities at CBS.

Years before I worked for television, I connected the medium with a deity. I spent the fall, winter, and spring of 1953–54 alone on an island in northern Minnesota, trying to write a novel which was cunningly set in the north woods. As a young man should be, I was sore at society and convinced that it was in decline.

My simile for this was the television set. I wrote that it "burned like the eye of God" into the living rooms and bedrooms and kitchens and dens and fishing shacks of people whose independence of judgment and taste had been swallowed up by this monster.

In March of that year, I shared a long bus ride with an elderly gentleman who had been a merchant seaman in World War II. He had sailed the north Atlantic. He had had ships torpedoed out from under him. I found this interesting and pressed him to tell me about it. He only wanted to discuss Liberace's Mother's Day television program of the previous year, which was more real to the old sea dog than his own peril on the deep.

E. B. White worried that radio's sound effects "are taking the place of sound itself." Television improved on this, imposing its own reality. A news editor told me years ago, "If it's not on 'The Evening News' it didn't happen." This was during Vietnam, which was called "the living room war."

It was bracing to be part of all this. I felt last night like the hero of a sci-fi movie, walking from the pyrotechnic world of network television into the black-and-white reality of retirement.

I used to be an active drunk, meaning a drunk who drinks. The drunk carries his action with him. He may be boring, but he is never bored. The prospect of sobriety scared me because I was afraid I would be bored, that life's party, drained of its excitement and vitality, would end.

I quit drinking. The black dog of boredom did not bite. I have been a busy fellow. In retirement, I will be less busy. Will I get bored?

❖ ❖ ❖ ❖ ❖

What I wanted was yesterday to be like any other day. That couldn't be.

Through the day, people stopped at my desk to wish me well. I didn't have much writing to do, although the broadcast had been extended to an hour because of the Persian Gulf War. I knew I was doing things for the last time as a staff writer for "The CBS Evening News."

Mike, working in Wisconsin, was not present, but Betty and the other children and I were called to the producer's office after the broadcast for cake, champagne, soft drinks, and complimentary remarks about me. I am as immodest as the next person, and I thought, I have left blood on the floor of this studio, and I may even deserve some of these pretty remarks.

Betty took the children and me to dinner uptown. I felt swell, as though I had won a race. We were a merry group. We asked a waiter to take our picture. Later Andrew said he heard people at a nearby table say, "Look at those nerdy tourists, having their picture taken."

❖ ❖ ❖ ❖ ❖

I went shopping with Betty this morning—just a few neighborhood stops: bank, post office, grocery, dry cleaner. It is liberating to shop on a weekday.

I read the *New York Times* today and *New York Newsday* and *Oggi America*. At work, I used to look through seven newspapers every day. I read some in *The House of Barrymore*. I listened to Verdi. I walked for an hour, down Central Park West, then along side streets.

It seemed a perfect first day of retirement, a Sunday without prospect of Monday.

I watched "The CBS Evening News." I wish we were reporting something beside the war. I don't believe anything I see or hear about the war, because we see and hear only what the generals want us to see and hear.

I have been asked if I would return, if the war drags on, to relieve any stressed-out colleagues on the evening news. I said I would do it, but I hope I do not have to go back. I have walked away from it.

Projects

One of the first things a retired man is supposed to do is tackle projects he had been putting off for years. Jobs await that his job made impossible to do. Often retirement gifts reflect his interests—a new set of car tools, a circular saw.

My retirement gifts certainly reflect my interests. They include tapes of *Dr. Strangelove* and the Olivier *Lear,* an autographed photograph of Paul Scofield, a WPA guide to Wisconsin, and a political T-shirt I wear as I write this.

The first project I must tackle, determined as a middle linebacker, is book control. After years of heedless breeding, books now litter our apartment in ungoverned congeries. I know there is nothing of the oily rag in this project, or the rich smell of loam, but it is a job I have been putting off until I retired, and it is symbolized by my bedside table, the site of an apparent book orgy.

Here's the problem: my bedside table measures sixteen inches by sixteen inches. On it, besides an alarm clock, is a scattershot collection of books, fallen into three stacks, twelve inches, sixteen inches, and twenty inches in height. The stacks just grew, in the mysterious manner by which books breed and travel.

The books are read, or partly read, or being reread. The titles change imperceptibly, as a volume from a bookstore or hall shelf wings into the room, crying, "Read me!" The oldest inhabitant of the table, by right of residence, probably is a leatherbound copy of Peter Alexander's edition of Shakespeare, which Betty bought me in England when she and her mother visited Cornwall and Devon in 1985.

There are three paperback editions of *Hamlet* on my table. What are they doing there? Stephen Booth's exasperating, exhilarating line-by-line annotation of the sonnets is at my ear. A biography of Nathanael West has replaced a biography of Delmore Schwartz.

One stack includes a volume of poetry by Amy Clampitt, *Miss Mackenzie* by Anthony Trollope, *The Global Marketplace* by Milton Moskowitz, and a Folger Library pamphlet, *The Bible in English, 1526–1611.*

I'm sure all this started with a one-volume, pre-Alexander edition of Shakespeare. An edition of Shakespeare was my first birthday present to Betty. We must own close to a dozen one-volume editions now. It always seems like a good idea to pick one up.

I don't know how many books I own about Shakespeare. The thought of counting them makes me ill. But I should rearrange them in some kind of order. That is a good retirement goal. How will I locate them? Stoll's *Art and Artifice in Shakespeare* made a break for it the other day and wound up next to *The Baseball Encyclopedia*, safe at home. Dover Wilson's *What Happens in Hamlet?* is cheek-to-cheek with Mencken's *Chrestomathy* on the journalism shelves.

Books are all over the place in this seven-and-a-half-room apartment. I cannot explain it. For those in similar circumstances, no explanation is necessary. For those who are not in such a predicament, no explanation will do.

Betty and I started out, like many Manhattan couples in the 1950s, with a few board-and-brick bookshelves. They bore a Shakespeare, a Bible, plays and novels of the day, and some of Betty's college books. ("Betty Drake, Swarthmore, 1955" is on the first page of Dostoevsky and Conrad, of Coleridge and Milton and others.) My Village books added to the collection, *The Autobiography of Alice B. Toklas, Ulysses,* Chekhov, the names taste of red wine and cheese.

The seed germinated much like Mr. Jefferson's Library, which became the Library of Congress. We have bookshelves in all the bedrooms, the living room, the dining room—shelves in all rooms except the kitchen and baths.

There are not enough shelves, so books lie on end tables and coffee tables and radiator tops. There are more than one hundred books on journalism. In the living room and hall are dozens of books about football, baseball, and boxing.

What's going to become of us?

Our children were starting college when the great Library of America series was born. We are charter subscribers, and now those volumes stretch on like Banquo's heirs. (But how else would I have read Parkman's *France and England in North America?* I remain an ignorant fellow, but less so.)

About a year ago, Betty and I went through the shelves as ruthlessly as Vikings and gathered a half dozen big cartons of books which we gave to charity. It did not seem to make a dent. No space opened up. I don't understand how this can be.

It is as though I acquired a flivver to fool around with in the garage, back in 1956, and now I open the door to a warehouse of cars, antique cars, cars of today, cars red or blue or black or gray or fuchsia, with parts stashed in corners, tires, carburetors, windshields, computers, rags, wrenches, compressors, shocks, all stacked to the ceiling, and where is that first flivver, how did I become possessed by this pastime?

In my few days of retirement, I have managed to shuffle books around, and my bedside table is clearer for the time. The Alexander Shakespeare is still there, along with just one *Hamlet,* a second-hand paperback edited by the great Kittredge. I don't know how I will find time to winnow the other books. When I worked in an office, I often felt that I met myself coming out the door as I returned home in the evening. I feel the same way in these first days of retirement. I fall behind, doing nothing.

❖ ❖ ❖ ❖ ❖

Groundhog Day came and went last Saturday, and I didn't have to write about it. How many times have I tried to think of something witty or novel to say over pictures of people clustered around a groundhog burrow, waiting for the rodent to emerge?

The fact that I thought about the event at all shows how little I am really retired. Perhaps I won't be retired until Groundhog Day rolls around and I won't think about what to write, or perhaps I will really be retired when I am actually curious about whether Punxsutawney Phil saw his shadow and discuss it with Betty. I hope I do not get that retired.

I made one of my infrequent appearances at church Sunday, accompanying Betty. The sermon was "Christian Attitudes Toward War and Peace." I hate the Gulf war. I do not know what it is about. The sermon encouraged me to maintain this opinion.

I learned this first week of retirement how comforted I am to be around Betty all day. She works in one room and I in another, but we are under the same roof, and we have lunch together, discussing mail and newspapers, and we are together at the cocktail hour and watch "The CBS Evening News" together before dinner.

Betty teaches children with learning disabilities. She sees them, one at a time, here in our apartment. She starts teaching early in the morning. I wake again to the patter of little feet. It is cheerful to have children in the apartment, even though they are not my own.

<u>Fever</u>

Wednesday, February 13

The hard worker who retired on Friday and died mowing the lawn on Saturday, before he could enjoy a single full day of retirement. . . .

We have all heard his story, an apprehensive chill climbing our spines. This is one reason why people are worried about retiring. They figure they have to keep on working to keep on living.

It embarrasses me to think that I might die, or even suffer a major illness, early in my retirement. I worry that my former colleagues might draw the wrong lesson from it. "Look at poor Mosedale," they might say. "Retired and dropped dead. Better not quit." (If only I could call from the grave: "Look, I drank and I smoked and no one in my family lives long!")

I began brooding about this more than a week ago when I went to bed for the night with a 99.9 fever, a trifle.

The thing is, I don't remember the time I last took my temperature. I was raised in a home where a thermometer was the device attached to the window, to tell you the temperature outdoors. Mother did not believe in fever thermometers, which she called "stuff and nonsense."

My sisters and I grew up hearing, "Go to bed with a cold and you'll be over it in two weeks. Go about your business and it will take you a fortnight." I must have been pretty young when I first heard this because it is how I learned the meaning of the word "fortnight." I have never missed a day of work because I had a fever.

Betty and I are improved enough that we kept a thermometer for the children, but I do not use it for myself. I took my temperature because I was thick-headed and cranky. I attributed this to a particularly long walk and a climb up six flights of stairs, carrying two six-packs of Diet Dr Pepper, all in the name of healthful exercise.

I have been seesawing with fever ever since, normal in the day, as high as 101.5 at night. I don't mind the effect, which is a little like drinking a couple of martinis, "loud-mouth soup," as we used to say at CBS Sports.

What's going on in the world makes better sense when viewed through the scarlet prism of a low fever; the Gulf war explained by generals with pointers, show-and-tell of so-called smart bombs, jubilation over alleged surgical strikes. The Alice-in-Wonderland quality of a fever makes cockeyed logic of this.

Struggling through my fever, I read a well-reasoned *Newsday* editorial supporting the war. It made no sense to me. Most of the *Newsday* columnists oppose the war. I hear the polls show the president enjoys the support of more than 90 percent of the American people. I take a walk for a few blocks and return to tell Betty, "I heard at least half a dozen people denounce the president and the Gulf war in harsh terms. What does that show?" She says, "It shows the Upper West Side of Manhattan is not the United States of America," a slice of truth that cuts through my fever.

During the day, with no fever, I read a story by a reporter who returned to El Salvador to find nothing changed after seventy-five thousand people were killed in ten years of war. That sounds like a fever dream, but it is reality.

I went to our neighborhood library the other day, the St. Agnes branch on Amsterdam Avenue. I do not often use the library, being a book-buyer, but I was researching facts about retirement. I found a notice on the door, saying that because of city budget cuts, the library will be closed on Saturdays as of April first, which seems to me a decision made by a bureaucrat with a high fever.

The fever broke and with it any concern I felt about psychological damage I might have inflicted on friends by dying early in retirement.

But before that happened, I had the first jounalistic anxiety dream of my retirement. It is two minutes to air. Lee Townsend gives me a blue index card, which we never used in the history of "The CBS Evening News." On it are scrawled sluglines for a dozen stories about which I know nothing. Lee tells me to write them before we go on air. I start to protest that this is impossible, and he says, "I can't talk now," which is the complete sentence most frequently heard in the newsroom. Panic wakes me up.

The old newsroom was always feverish. It was like New York. It never shut down. It was a dream-maker.

A producer once dreamed that he and a colleague were ordered to hustle down to Washington, driving backward. Lee dreamed he was assassinated by the terrorist we all knew would one day invade the newsroom. As Lee lay dying, he gasped, "Don't lead with it."

I dreamed one night that we inexplicably ran out of copy with ten minutes left in the broadcast. An executive cried, "Go to 'The Battle Hymn of the Republic'!" I rose to protest, but then I saw on every monitor in the newsroom, dozens of monitors, a choir, a gorgeous young woman in army uniform leading the voices, I heard the words and the music swelling. . . .

The fever is gone. I wonder if retirement means the anxiety dreams are gone, too.

When I told Andy Rooney last summer that I was going to retire at the end of the year, he said he wanted to give a party for me. I suppose I thought that was a nice thing for Andy to say. I should have known better. If Andy says he is going to do something, he does it.

We were all busy being busy, and then Andy asked me to put together a guest list of about forty people, which I did, and then the invitation arrived in the mail, a handsome, hand-written invitation for cocktails and dinner at "a gathering of some friends of John Mosedale on the occasion of his giving up gainful employment." The date was February 22, the place a club on the East Side.

The hosts were Judy Hole and Andy. The three of us worked together on a program called "Calendar," back in the early 1960s, and we have stayed in touch.

The date engraved itself on my mind. A couple of weeks ago, I began to think about the evening seriously. Pretty soon, I awoke in the night, thinking about it. It would pop into my mind while I was walking, listening to my Aiwa. The date began to seem like the date for a job interview.

I was worrying about what I would say at my dinner. I knew I would be called on for a few words. I am a gabby fellow, but I am not a public speaker. I figured we would be hearing from Andy, Walter Cronkite, Harry Reasoner, and Ray Gandolf, who speak for a living. (Dan Rather would not attend, being called to Saudi Arabia.)

I did not want to embarrass my family, my friends, or myself. In a way, it was harder that this was a gathering of friends. If you are verbose and stupid in front of strangers, the consolation is that you may never have to see them again. (Consider the keynote speaker at our great political conventions.)

I thought wildly back to my extreme youth. When I was in preschool, the teachers put me off in a corner at lunch because I was given to storytelling that so gripped my little comrades that they forgot to eat. In the fourth and fifth grades, I was called on by teachers to fill slack times with a *Bildungsroman* about a haunted house, to which I gave a street address for realism.

But the monologist's gift, if that's what it was, is gone.

In my speech, I could view the future of network television news with alarm. The other day, I learned that the executive producer and the senior producer of "The CBS Evening News" had been fired. The broadcast, rated first for decades, now sometimes finished in third place. In television as in sports, management fires the field manager. Ratings are a strange way to judge a news broadcast, but that is the name of the game we play.

What I could worry about in my speech is the talk heard in the corridors and in the press that network managements want cheaper, friendlier news. I would then sound like every other retired person who decries the direction the company is taking, complains about younger executives, says if only old J.B. were here. I would be every retired ballplayer, actor, or fighter who says, hand on heart, "They just don't have it *here* anymore."

There would be people in the audience, moreover, who knew far more than I did about corporate policy.

A novice with a speech to make is like someone facing elective surgery, abstracted and angry. I anticipated this evening when my friends would gather. If it just weren't for that speech. . . .

What if I offered some upbeat advice about retirement? It would not come from my limited experience, but from books I have been reading at the library. In *The Aging Game: Success, Sanity and Sex After 50,* Barbara Gallatin Anderson writes about a tiny, eighty-year-old woman who, mauled by her drunken, two-hundred-pound husband, climbed up from bed and threw him out the window.

Asked how she did it, she said, "Easy. I got angry."

Mrs. Anderson advises the elderly to get angry. Well, that's not advice I want to be handing out at my retirement dinner. Besides, I don't feel elderly. I don't mind being called old. I prefer to think of myself as chronologically challenged.

What gets me angry are the cutbacks at the St. Agnes library, where I found *The Aging Game.*

I could tell listeners that in three weeks I've already learned the joy of waking in the morning and knowing that I do not have to leave the apartment. I can listen to Shakespeare or Sinatra anytime I feel like it, for as long as I feel like it. I walk for an hour, look at the people, look at the grand old apartment buildings. That about exhausts my retirement as subject matter, not at all the stuff of a compelling speech.

In the end, at my retirement party, after the cocktail hour and the dinner, after remarks by Andy and Judy and Walter and Harry and Ray and Betty's sister, Barbara, I stood on my feet and talked about the great fortune of being a newspaperman and a television writer, how important I thought the work was, just getting the names right, and how much fun I had, and how grateful I was that all of them were present.

I guess the speech went all right. I was not much of a judge of that, my eyes misted with joy through the evening. I have had no doubt that I did the right thing, retiring when I did, and this festive time seemed to confirm it. How wonderful people are! I thought. How warm and thoughtful! There are not many times when I feel this kind of universal sympathy.

Our children were there, Mike back from Wisconsin for the occasion. For the first time they saw in person some of the people I had worked with for years.

Retirement parties are supposed to be bittersweet for the person who is retiring, looking forward to leisure, looking back with a pang at finished work and lost colleagues. I felt nothing but joy. I had said goodbye to my work a month earlier. Betty and I weren't going anywhere. I could visit with my friends at the party just about any time.

I never saw the evening's only cloud. Lee made a brief and funny speech. What he didn't say was that he had just been fired. He was on his way out of the building to the party when he was told. He sat through the evening of my party without a word of what had happened to him.

A friend called this morning and told me Lee had been fired. So many people at CBS News have been fired over the past few years that I thought I was beyond shock, but I cannot imagine anyone who has worked with Lee who will not be shocked by this development.

I already have heard three theories. One is that the company, like many other companies these days, wants to get rid of higher priced, veteran employees and replace them with younger people whose salaries are lower. Another theory is that "The Evening News" does not want people around who are too close to Dan. Another theory is that CBS News does not want people around with memories of the way things used to be done.

I don't know that any of those theories is true. I never paid attention to front office politics. I cannot think of a reason for firing Lee that makes sense to anyone interested in producing the best kind of news broadcast. For the time I worked there, Lee was the most respected figure on "The CBS Evening News."

I cannot reach Lee. His line is busy. He will be taking a lot of calls.

Finding Time

Saturday, March 16

Trying to write and farm at the same time, E. B. White learned the only way he could get any writing done was to stay in his pajamas and stay in bed. Once he was dressed, he got busy with farming.

Pascal said he had discovered "that all unhappiness of men comes from one single fact, that they cannot stay quietly in their own room."

The recognitions of White and Pascal are the only explanations I can find for the spooky ease with which time passes in my retirement. I believe that by the time anyone is sixty-five years old, he should have found more than enough to do during the day without going to the office, the factory—or the farm.

I am far less resourceful than many people. My range of interests is narrow. I play no games—golf, tennis, or bowling. I don't hunt or fish. I don't drive a car, skate, or ski. I buy a lot of books in a disorganized manner, but I don't "collect" books, or anything else.

I wouldn't know what to write if I were asked to list my hobbies. Reading? Listening to music? I suppose those count, although they are the sort of choices made by beauty pageant contestants, along with "believes in world peace."

The sports I played are the games of youth—football, softball, sparring. I love to walk, but I walk in the spirit of Thoreau, who said, " . . . the walking of which I speak has nothing in it akin to exercise, as it is called, as the sick take medicine at stated hours—or the swinging of dumbbells."

I have never found a better place to walk than New York City. I have walked its miles ever since I arrived here thirty-seven years ago, and I have not yet exhausted the resources of my neighborhood. I plan in retirement to take a bus or subway downtown, disembark when I feel like it, and wander through whatever section of the city is at hand, from Columbus Circle to the Battery—the theater district, the garment district, Chelsea, the Village, Little Italy, Chinatown, Foley Square, the waterfront.

These places all are as dear to me as a walk in the woods. They hold surprises. I have not visited some of them for years. The homeless, the drunk, the junkie, the menacing are painted out in my memory. My portraits of the city are idealized. I am not an optimist about many things, but I believe the city will survive the ominous times our country lives in.

I read that most retired people retire to the places where they have been living. It would be sad to spend your working life someplace you want to leave. All I need to do is to walk a few blocks to understand why I don't want to retire anywhere else.

Retirement has robbed me of a stroll that filled me with wonder. I would walk out of the Broadcast Center in the evening, over to Ninth Avenue, up the street past Roosevelt Hospital, the big church of St. Paul the Apostle, past Fordham University at Lincoln Center, with the Empire Hotel and O'Neal's Balloon on my right, turn left, walk through the plaza past the lighted fountain between the New York State Theater and Avery Fisher Hall and meet Betty in front of the Metropolitan Opera.

That was about a fifteen-minute walk from my place of work. I never got over that—rising from my desk and the world of consumer prices, floods, or a crazy with a gun, and going to the opera.

Betty and I saw *Rosenkavalier* the other night, as President Bush, elsewhere, announced the end of the Gulf war. The shooting started the night Betty and I watched Faust seduce Marguerite and pay for it. We took the Columbus Avenue bus from home to *Rosenkavalier*. I walked from work to *Faust*. The Gulf war took place, for us, between work and retirement, between two operas.

In retirement, I have taken to dreaming about my novel. I wonder if I will write it. I have written a few unpublished novels. I am not passionate about this. Perhaps that is the problem. The novelist should be willing to sacrifice his mother for a novel, as Faulkner said, or give up children, as Mencken suggested. Well, that's okay if you are Proust or Joyce, but I am Mosedale.

Ten years ago or more, Betty and I were canoeing in the twilight in a little lake near our summer place. We were quiet. The forest murmured with a light breeze high in the pines. There was the occasional splash of a fish jump. It was a warm night.

We wore bathing suits, and I watched the movement of Betty's back, the fall of her hair on her white skin in the dusk. Then the full moon climbed above the edge of pines which were black against the night sky. It seemed a bigger moon than I had ever seen, looming, a moon bigger than the earth, a moon out of fantasy.

And the idea for the novel came to me. I could just about hear dialogue that extended over decades. The novel has nothing to do with a moonrise, or with an aging couple on a lake.

❖ ❖ ❖ ❖ ❖

The other day I made my first visit to the main reading room of the New York Public Library since it was computerized. Soon there may be no need for the marble extravaganza which celebrates a past confident enough in the future to invest time and money in a building to house books. We may not need books. They will all be stored on computer chips, in a shoe box, if we still have feet.

The computers, which are basic enough for me to operate, list all books catalogued since 1972. Books catalogued before that year are listed on file cards in bound volumes along the wall.

I enter the name *William Shakespeare.* The computer tells me there are six hundred items under that name. By hitting the return key, I can find a call number for each item.

I enter my name. I find three items. I am immortal, libraryized.

I enter *retire.* Nothing. I type *retirement.* Four hundred and forty items. Retirement is a little better than two-thirds as compelling a subject as Shakespeare.

I choose two titles, hoping to find out where the time goes.

Looking Forward: A Guide for Retirement by Mordun Lazarus informs me that a worker who devotes retirement hours to volunteer activities is happier than a rich fellow who spends his hours getting drunk. It seems to me that depends.

Lazarus says, "Some gerontologists believe that you reach your full intellectual potential in your sixties and seventies." I take this to mean that I have time to learn not to do so many dumb things.

The second book I looked at was *Breaking Patterns: Redesigning Your Later Years* by Catherine Anderson Pacheco. She and her husband retired to a yacht. I don't believe that is a profitable avenue for me to explore. I'm afraid I would be bored on a yacht, although I enjoyed sea life when I was in the navy. But I was twenty years old.

My belief persists that I will have more trouble finding time than filling it.

I recently made my first visit to the Motor Vehicle Bureau. I need a New York State ID card, which is a driver's license for people who don't drive. Some years ago I encountered a hotel clerk who dismissed my CBS employee card, my CBS News card, and all my credit cards. She demanded a driver's license. Betty had her driver's license with her, so we escaped prison, but I vowed then to get the state ID card.

The Motor Vehicle Bureau is way downtown on Worth Street, not far from the courthouses. I know the area from jury duty. I also walked there years ago on my circuitous returns from the waterfront, where I worked, to the Village, where I played.

I continue to feel nostalgic about the area, although I no longer regard every messenger and clerk as figures to be envied because they appear to have always lived in New York.

The waiting line was impressive, even by city standards, stretching perhaps a block and a half and doubling on itself. I was pleased I had not tried to do this when I was working.

I completed my application, paid the money, had my picture taken. I called the CBS barber shop and made an appointment for midafternoon. I walked the walk I used to walk, a *boulevardier* on Sixth Avenue. The scene is both different and the same, like me.

I came upon an art deco diner. I ate a hamburger and read the newspaper while listening to Billie Holiday on the juke box, nothing but Billie.

I cannot find the time, just looking and listening, for all there is to do.

Parsifal

Betty and I saw *Parsifal* at the Metropolitan Opera last night, and thinking about the production in the small hours, I found the answer to a mystery that has puzzled me since 1956.

I don't mean I was haunted by the mystery. It was only a question that popped into my head at unpredictable intervals. Now retirement provides me with time to think about the inconsequential.

Parsifal by my watch ran five hours and forty minutes last night, which is a lot of Wagner or anyone else. It is about an hour longer, for example, than the production of an uncut

Hamlet, and an uncut *Hamlet* is supposed to be too long for today's distracted audience to bear.

I don't think many people, even maddened Wagnerites, would regard *Parsifal* as a date opera, that is, an opera to which you take a young woman after you've just become interested in her. *La Traviata* and *Tosca,* these are date operas.

My mystery was: why did I take Betty to hear *Parsifal* at the old Met at a Saturday matinee, March 13, 1956, about two months after I met her?

I later learned that this was the first opera she had ever seen. Like virtually everything else in my life, our date was complicated by the fact that I was drinking in those days. I suffered from a terrible vertigo. Drink seemed to cure it, but I couldn't very well ask Betty to come to the Blarney Stone while I threw back three or four vodkas, so, sober and dizzy, I clung to her as we climbed up and up and up to the only seats I could afford on my shipping clerk's salary, and I held her hand or put my arm around her during the long afternoon. She said to herself, "He really must like me." I did, but I held her for support, as the vertiginous will understand.

Why *Parsifal?* It is not exactly an opera that explains itself. It couldn't have meant anything to her. I at least knew the plot line.

The only thing stranger than the workings of a young man's mind are the workings of an old man's mind.

I learned late last summer that the Met was putting together this new production of *Parsifal* with Placido Domingo. Betty and I already had received our season tickets, and we had overlooked *Parsifal.* I sent for tickets. I found a place where I could buy the opera on records, ten sides, the 1962 Bayreuth Festival recording. I bought the libretto. I Xeroxed the review of the production Betty and I had seen in 1956. It turned out we had seen a new production back then. Howard Taubman in the *Times* called it "an effort to bring *Parsifal* into the present." He found this attempt "only partly successful." I hadn't remembered.

I gave the record, the libretto, and the review to Betty for our wedding anniversary, which is December 22. We had plenty of time to prepare for last night's performance.

Betty and I enjoyed a leisurely dinner at home, laughing over our memories of our first *Parsifal,* and made our way by bus down Columbus Avenue. We settled into our seats well before the first strains of the prelude, sitting in the fifth row of the orchestra, a long way from the last row in the upper reaches of the old house.

Later last night, or to be accurate, early this morning, I solved the old mystery of why on that gray winter day in 1956 I took Betty to see this particular opera, this unlikely choice. It was rooted in a time before I knew Betty, a moment in solitude when I looked across a silent north woods snow and envisioned an unknown woman.

❖ ❖ ❖ ❖ ❖

I met Betty at about seven o'clock in the evening of January 12, 1956. That hour was as early as I could make it. I worked as a shipping clerk near the waterfront, off Peck Slip, pouring foul chemicals into barrels. At the end of the day, I scrubbed with kerosene to remove tars. Then I hustled back to my place on MacDougall Street and washed off the kerosene.

Betty had invited me to dinner. She was living, with two older women, in the house where Emily Post grew up, on Tenth Street, off Fifth Avenue, one million miles from my seedy digs.

I rang the doorbell that January night with no special sense of destiny. I caught my first glimpse of Betty, a shadow, through the frosted window as she answered the door. I stepped into the vestibule. She stood there, with her blue eyes and light brown hair, slim in her sleeveless silver lamé blouse and dark velvet skirt.

We drank martinis, Betty, the two older women, and I. Betty had cooked dinner, a sliced mushroom dish. It was a pleasant evening. I suppose that when I left the house, I thought that was all it was. She seemed so young to me! I am seven years older than she is.

I thought of her as a family friend. Our families both spent summers on a little island in northern Minnesota, but she and I hadn't met. Her family rented the cabin next to ours in the summer of 1945. I was away in the navy when Betty met my mother, my sisters, and my little Scottie.

Her father bought a cabin in the next bay in 1946, the summer I got out of the navy. I accompanied a friend to their cabin while he asked Betty's sister for a date, and when Barbara stepped on the porch I saw this kid sister in the recesses of the living room, but I paid no attention to her.

I went off to the University of Wisconsin, attending more or less the year-around, which more than my intellect explains how I graduated in two and a half years. In 1948, Betty's father joined the economic AID mission to Greece, and except for one summer, they did not come to the island for six years.

And so in 1956 I dined with this family friend because Barbara, married and living in Connecticut, hearing I was in the Village, told Betty we should all get together. I didn't have a telephone, being uncivilized, so Betty sent me a Christmas card, with the invitation.

(Eventually, I tired of explaining how Betty and I met in big, wicked New York and not on our bucolic island, so I came to say she approached me in a Village restaurant with an unlit cigarette and said, "Set me on fire, baby." The number of people who believed this story explains a good deal about election results.)

Something called me back to call on her after our dinner. I should have known: I had remembered what she wore when we met.

I was so in love with New York that I didn't think I had love left over for anything else. My job paid for my books, meals, newspapers, magazines, theater and opera tickets, and beer. I had girlfriends. That was no problem in the Village in the '50s. I was sure I would never find a woman who would want to live in New York and in a north woods cabin with an outhouse. New York entertained me, challenged me, and protected me from responsibility. I thought of myself as a self-contained unit.

Betty was coming off a broken romance. We started going together, first weekly, then more often. In the beginning, I believed I was an older friend of the family, steering a young girl around the city. Betty thought of me that way, too.

I took her out to dinner. I took her to see *He Who Gets Slapped,* in an off-Broadway production. After the show, she said, "Let's go someplace and talk about this." On a brisk winter night, we rode the Staten Island Ferry and walked to Chinatown for dinner and walked home to the Village. We saw *The Threepenny Opera* at the Theatre De Lys. We made angel wings in the snow in Washington Square Park and sat, just the two of us, late at night in the park, feeling safe. That's how long ago it was.

We discussed everything—politics, religion, children, tastes—before we realized we were talking about us. We ate spaghetti and drank red wine in Village joints and sauerbraten and beer in Yorktown and we watched Floyd Patterson knock out Archie Moore on television at the Neutral Corner Bar and Grill. We saw Jason Robards in *The Iceman Cometh* at the Circle in the Square, and it was one of the best evenings I ever spent in the theater.

We rode the subway to Coney and to Far Rockaway, where we undressed under the boardwalk and left our clothes and money there while we swam in the Atlantic under a night sky.

We became a couple, lustful and happy, kissing our mouths bloody in the summer nights.

Betty was lovely, intelligent, and sweet. She was direct. She did not talk the jargon of the day, overheard Freud or borrowed bop.

Her parents were concerned about Betty and me. I was working on the waterfront, a job with no prospects, looking toward renewing my life in news. Russ thought of me as a writer, meaning I would carry his daughter off to starve in a garret while I sweated over pentameters. My mother approved since Betty and I were both islanders.

In July, after a day of sun and seafood at Jones Beach, Betty and I saw a ghastly production of the great musical *Showboat,* and between acts, I proposed and slipped an engagement ring on Betty's finger.

In October, I found the job of my dreams, writing for the North American Newspaper Alliance, or NANA, which was located in the *Times* building. My first week there, Betty and I attended the world premiere of *The Ten Commandments,* Betty in a strapless gown, I in a tux, searchlights painting the sky over Broadway. The movie was tacky, although Seventh Commandment pencils sold briskly, but the occasion proved to me that I had the girl, the job—I was making 120 smackeroos a week—and I didn't need anything more.

We were married in the Little Church Around the Corner. Our honeymoon was two nights at the Plaza. You can't beat that. We woke up the morning after our marriage to discover a pigeon had laid an egg on our windowsill.

Betty found our first apartment, one room with a tiny kitchen and bath on the Upper West Side. The day after Sputnik went up, we moved to the ground-floor apartment next door, three rooms with a backyard, all the space we would ever need.

We loved each other, and we loved babies. Amy was born ten months after we were married, then Laura, Andrew, and Michael—four babies in six years. This is how Betty is: I had just started working in television when a bad situation came up at work. I was asked to do something I didn't think I should do. I told Betty, "I'm going to resign." She was just home from the hospital with a brand-new baby, giving us two children. We had about $4.75 in the bank. She said, "You do what you think is right." (The problem at the office corrected itself.)

After each of our children was born, the doctor said about Betty, "That is quite a woman you have there."

During her first pregnancy, not long after we were married, I noticed that when she crawled out of bed in the middle of the night she muttered, "Drat!" I thought, I am married to a woman who says "Drat!" She also said, and says, "Shoot!" I suppose I found this endearing because the words were Betty's expletives, her own, at a time when advanced young women slipped into the kind of below-decks language designed to prove they were one of the boys.

She was neither prude nor wet blanket. There was a song of my youth, the refrain of which ran, "I hung around with evil companions, and I had a wonderful time." So I did. Betty gamely sat in the morning with me and Village companions who were drunk or stoned; she accompanied me to Baltimore and Philadelphia, Los Angeles and San Francisco on football weekends; she cooked meals for unexpected guests I brought home.

When my drinking got out of hand, Betty lived with it. She told me, the eternal and truthful refrain of a drunk's wife, that I was killing myself. I assured her I would not do that. I told her I was not destined for a drunkard's grave. I wasn't, but it was a near thing and I was lucky. Betty never screamed at me, or threatened to leave me or to kick me out. She managed, sometimes, to make her anger and anxiety clear to me. She marked liquor bottles in an effort to keep an eye on my intake. If she cried about my drinking, I never saw it.

She attended AlAnon meetings for families of drunks, around the time I started going to Alcoholics Anonymous. She wound up addressing a big AlAnon-AA joint session. Afterwards, an official came up to her and said, "You are *mensch.*" Ah, I thought, but she is also The Woman.

After our children were in school, Betty did some volunteer teaching. Then she attended Teachers College at Columbia University, earning a master's degree in education. Betty did all of this without interrupting her job of running a household.

A friend asked me not long ago if Betty and I fight. We don't. I recall two big blowups in thirty-five years of marriage. Once it was her fault. Both times I left the house for a couple of hours until I cooled off. You don't spend much time in close quarters without being able to collect a few grievances, if you are a grievance collector. I believe these are un-important, measured against love and sleeping pulse-to-pulse and should be ignored.

I entered into marriage with three important pieces of advice. One was from a popular song: "For every little fault you have, I have a dozen more." One was from my sister Anne: "Sometimes you have to keep your mouth shut." One was from Father Randolph Ray, who married us: " 'Never let the sun set on thy wrath.' "

I am not complacent about any of this. Betty and I could become the battling Bickersons tomorrow. I doubt that this will happen, but I do not take my wife for granted.

Another thing. I am much more romantic than Betty. I believe in the lyrics of the old popular songs. I believe in "The Way You Look Tonight" and "All the Things You Are" and "Always." I believe you never really get to know another person; it takes a lifetime just to get close.

She goes along with me when I talk like this, but I can tell she is more realistic and less the cornball. "Across my life," breathes the dying Cyrano, "one whispering, silken gown." How great! I thought when I first read that line in high school. How true! I still feel that way.

Last night, thinking of *Parsifal,* and the odd personal mystery, I found the answer as in a dream. I remembered the late winter of 1954. I was alone in the cabin on the island in northern Minnesota, as I had been since September, writing and reading, walking and thinking.

It is a Saturday afternoon. The purple sky is low, threatening sleet or snow, but for the first time in months it is warm enough for me to do a hand laundry in the unheated room where we eat in the summer.

I am listening to the Metropolitan Opera on radio. The opera is *Parsifal.*

The day promises spring even under the threatening sky. I imagine a woman I had never seen. Two years later, I met her and took her to her first opera.

Better than Being President
Friday, March 29

"Most of the rewards of the Presidency, in these degenerate days, have come to be very trashy."

So wrote H. L. Mencken in 1931, and things have only gotten worse. But we insist on regarding the office as an honor bestowed, and so I wondered how, if our jobs define us, does a president handle retirement?

Today, of course, the president is a celebrity, and he retires into celebrity with a swollen pension and more bodyguards than an emir.

I was curious to learn how nineteenth-century presidents retired, back when they retired into the crowd with the rest of us. I don't mean great men like Jefferson. I mean the sort of presidents who served between, say, Lincoln and Theodore Roosevelt, run-of-the-mill presidents of the kind we have been electing.

In the great golden reading room of the New York Public Library, I looked through *The Presidents' Last Years: George Washington to Lyndon B. Johnson* by Homer Cunningham. The subtitle set me to brooding about Darwin, but then I turned to stories about Rutherford B. Hayes, Chester A. Arthur, Benjamin Harrison, and Grover Cleveland, three Republicans, one Democrat, none on anyone's list of ten greatest presidents.

None of them retired rich. All went to work on leaving the White House, as lawyers or businessmen. Arthur was ill of kidney disease when he retired from the presidency, and he died two years later, but until then he lent his name to his old law firm and made public appearances when he was up to it.

These presidents did not even have Social Security, and they retired without pensions. Andrew Carnegie wanted to give Cleveland a gratuity as "a rememberance" when Cleveland departed Gomorrah on the Potomac. Cleveland declined on the grounds that it would be improper to accept money that way. (Recent presidents have overcome such scruples, if they ever had them, but then Mencken called Cleveland "a good man in a bad trade.")

Arthur, Harrison, Cleveland, Hayes—none of these hardworking, retired presidents ever spoke of missing the White House and its attendant glories. I can already tell from the way people ask me about my retirement that they expect me to say I miss the job I loved doing, but, in truth, I don't.

The late-nineteenth-century world of the presidents I have been studying was in many ways a harsher world than our own. The contrasts between wealth and poverty were as extreme as they are today, and there was no welfare system. The poor were ignored. Armies of children slept in the streets and fields. Child labor was legal and encouraged. Lynching was illegal but popular. Social Darwinism prevailed.

In this group of undistinguished ex-presidents, Rutherford B. Hayes has given me the most to think about as a retired man. What I knew about him was what I learned in school. He was elected president although Samuel Tilden received more popular votes. Mrs. Grider in fifth grade used this election in a vain attempt to help her students understand the electoral college. The other thing about Hayes is that his wife was called "Lemonade Lucy" because she would not allow liquor to be served in the White House.

According to Cunningham, Hayes in retirement rose well above the mediocrity of his presidency. He labored for his fellow Civil War veterans. He was a working trustee of two colleges. He believed education was the only way former slaves could rise in society and he raised money for their schools, visiting the South to see the work carried out.

He maintained, without the help of taxpayer-financed secretaries, a vast correspondence with politicians, scholars, and businessmen. Hayes rose early and "tried to get the distasteful work done before breakfast." He and Lucy, college graduates with "rather cosmopolitan tastes," spent much of the day reading and discussing biography and history. They enjoyed Browning and Emerson.

In retirement, this conservative nineteenth-century Republican became convinced that crime was "largely a problem arising out of poverty." He called himself a nihilist, saying that by nihilism he meant "the essence of the Declaration of Independence and the Sermon on the Mount."

Hayes attacked what he called "the wrong and evils of the money-piling tendency of our country . . . giving all power to the rich and bringing in pauperism and wretchedness like a flood."

He used his retirement to work and think and he seemed to have a good time doing so.

Retirement Life and Death

Wednesday, April 17

I've been tackling the basic retirement job the past couple of weeks: cleaning out the garage.

We don't have a garage so what I've been cleaning out is the room that is my study. It is the first bedroom as you enter the apartment, next to the bathroom. Betty and I shared this smallish room when we moved into the apartment in 1961. Since then all four of the children have occupied the room at various times, but now it serves as my study.

In spite of all my hard work these past weeks, the room inspector would find no difference in the way the place looks. All is clutter, including a half dozen cardboard boxes full of stuff, much of it belonging to Betty's mother and moved here when she entered a nursing home last year. Some of the stuff is mine.

My progress is hidden. I have emptied the file cabinets, which serve as desk drawers. I refilled them with matter I might need. I have gotten rid of enough paper to circle the globe or reach Mars, one of those statistics.

Out went eighteen years' worth of desk calendars, records of appointments, show times, party dates, even sluglines of news stories I wrote. It is shocking to find proof that events that seem to have taken place in the recent past occurred more years ago than I am likely to have years left me.

Newspapers shed clippings as birds shed feathers. I dispatched dispatches I had clipped but not mailed years ago to children at college or to friends. I couldn't bear to part with some of the clippings, although my *New York Times* transcript of Richard Nixon's last news conference was not much more than dust.

We have been experiencing record heat since I last attacked this journal. It hit ninety one day last week, as Betty, the girls, Andrew, and I ate a picnic in Central Park. We sat under a tree that offered little shade, since the leaves were not yet out.

Joggers circled the reservoir in the heat. Some of them looked like retired fellows. Jogging is not a pursuit for this retired fellow. It is no fun for me. How pleasant retirement is, I think, as I drift along, justified by projects.

Then Monsieur Mercade paid his call. We got word that Betty's Uncle Clarke died. He was eighty-six years old and had suffered various ailments, but until recently he was vigorous, his mind sharp and his voice strong.

He was, like Betty's parents, a Kansan, and although he had not lived there for more than half a century, the state shaped his accent. Betty's mother was visiting us in 1988 when the University of Kansas won the national basketball championship. She and I watched the championship game on television, and afterwards we called Uncle Clarke to congratulate him. He was pretty excited. He recalled playing in the KU band.

"I studied with Professor Naismith, you know," he said. The professor taught a hygiene course at KU, aimed chiefly at convincing young men not to sleep with a woman until they were married. "As I recall," Uncle Clarke said, "it didn't do much good."

We will miss Clarke. He was gentle and amusing. He spoke at a memorial service after Russ died, recalling his brother-in-law as an optimist about the nation and in lesser matters. " 'You'd miss a lot of golf if you took the weather reports too seriously,' Russ said."

Betty canceled her appointments with students and drove to Washington for her uncle's services. It was hard for her to tell her mother about Clarke's death. He had been married to Helen's sister, who died fifteen years ago, and he and Helen had known each other since high school.

A few days after Betty returned, she and I dined with a group that might be called "CBS News in Exile," former workers on "The CBS Evening News" who recently left the company. We shared laughter and memories over analgesics and a gorgeous, unhealthful feast at an hour when all of us used to be stretched on the rack, then attended a one-man show about Huey Long which reminded us that even demagoguery is in a state of decline.

It was the fifth day in a row Betty and I had attended something theatrical. The string included a ghastly *Romeo and Juliet* at the Juilliard School, where we have seen good things. *Women in Shakespeare* at Juilliard the following day was an improvement, but it seems a wonder that someone can attend drama school for three years and still not learn that princesses do not stride like American coeds late for a bio exam and that queens should stand straight.

We saw *The Taming of the Shrew,* a seldom-performed opera by a fellow named Vittorio Gianinni, who was born in this country and had heard Puccini. The opera ended in a duet that left us in tears. "Why didn't they warn us?" Betty asked indignantly.

The *Shrew,* staged at the Manhattan School of Music with a ticket price of fifteen dollars, was praised in the same issue of the *Daily News* that called *Miss Saigon,* at fifty dollars a ticket, "Viet Numb . . . vulgar, drab and tacky." The tourist or the uninitiated New Yorker is unaware of shows like the *Shrew* and so holds a diminished view of the theater scene.

Our entertainment orgy ended with the Jupiter Symphony playing Mozart and Schumann. For all of that, these days were a reminder that retirement does not free you from the realities of sickness and death. Retirement is real life, with the office left out.

Will and I
Tuesday, April 23

This is the day William Shakespeare's birthday is celebrated, at least by me, and in the sloth of retirement I did not buy one red rose. But I thought of Shakespeare today; you can be sure of that. Not a day of my life passes that I don't think of Shakespeare and it is a rare and wasted day when I do not read something by him.

There is a *New Yorker* cartoon showing a drunk in his living room, glass in hand, smiling foggily at a bust of Shakespeare and saying, "Philosopher, playwright, knower of men, colleague, pal o' mine." That is how I, sober, feel about Shakespeare.

I get a little crazy when I think about Shakespeare. So does everyone else. A few years back, a business newsletter printed something to the effect that Shakespeare was the smartest person who ever lived. I was instantly asked by a number of people who knew of my passion for Shakespeare if I agreed. How would I know? Who am I to say? For all I know, the smartest person who ever lived may be selling fish in Seoul, South Korea.

I don't read Shakespeare and listen to him and look at his plays because he was smart, although he clearly was. Intelligence is only one in a list of human virtues and not necessarily the most important. If I were only looking for intelligence, I'd be whiling away my evenings with Alfred North Whitehead.

Shakespeare is my writer of writers. I think there is Shakespeare and then there is everybody else. I know, I know he could write badly. There is a line in *King John* I wish he had crossed out.

Friends may say I talk about Shakespeare a lot, which is not true. I seldom speak of him, except in response to a question or a comment, because I am afraid of sounding weird. What goes on between Will and me is private.

Harold Bloom, coauthor of *The Book of J,* says, "It's not just that Shakespeare gives us most of our representations of cognition as such. I'm not so sure he didn't largely invent what we think of as cognition. I remember saying something like this to a seminar consisting of professional teachers of Shakespeare, and one of them got very indignant and said, 'You are confusing Shakespeare with God.' I don't see why one shouldn't, so to speak." Now if I were articulate enough to say something like that, people would be checking my mouth for foam.

I walk out of this room, a few feet down the hall, and I find nine rows of bookshelves, each shelf a little more than four feet long.

On part of one shelf are the Pocket Book/Modern Library editions of Shakespeare's plays, sonnets, and narrative poems, arranged in the order in which they might have been written.

Occupying part of the space above them is a mix of Signet Classic and New Penguin paperbacks of the plays, arranged alphabetically. On part of the shelf above that are the Arden editions of the plays, also arranged alphabetically. ("Those are the keepsake editions," we heard a young fellow say to his lass one evening at Shakespeare & Co., a local bookstore.)

I've read each of these editions, and others, at least once. On another group of shelves, the following titles catch my eye:

Broken Nuptials in Shakespeare's Plays by Carol Thomas Neely; *Impressions of Shakespeare,* British Academy Lectures, edited by Kenneth Muir; *A Companion to Shakespeare Studies 1937,* edited by Harley Granville-Barker and G. B. Harrison; *Hamlet—A New Version* by Rouben Manoulian (the most-discussed play in history is in need of constant improvement); *The Great Feast of Language in Love's Labour's Lost* by William C. Carroll.

Representing Shakespeare: New Psychoanalytic Essays, edited by Murray Schwartz and Coppelia Kahn; *Shakespeare Our Contemporary* by Jan Kott; *Romeo and Juliet—A Motion Picture Edition,* produced for Metro-Goldwyn-Mayer by Irving J. Thalberg, directed by George Cukor, adapted for the screen by Talbot Jennings, 1936; *Othello, A New Variorum Edition,* edited by Horace Howard Furness Jr., a Dover Press republication of the 1886 edition; *Macbeth,* ditto except the variorum originally was published in 1873; *Othello* in a French translation; *Othello* as planned for production at the Moscow Art Theatre by Konstantin Stanislavsky; *The Woman's Part: Feminist Criticism of Shakespeare,* edited by Carolyn Ruth Swift Lenz, Gayle Greene and Carol Thomas Neely; *The Life of Shakespeare* by Frank Harris.

Shakespeare's Game by William Gibson; *A Cry of Players,* which is a play about Shakespeare by Gibson; *The Book Known as Q* by Robert Giroux; *The Hamlet Letters of Henry Miller; What Happens in Hamlet* by J. Dover Wilson; *The Fifteen-Minute Hamlet* by Tom Stoppard; *Hamlet and the Philosophy of Literary Criticism* by Morris Weitz; *Aspects of Shakespeare's "Problem Plays,"* edited by Kenneth Muir and

Stanley Wells; *Shakespeare's English Kings: History, Chronicle and Drama* by Peter Saccio; *Shakespeare's Festive Comedy* by C. L. Barber; *That Shakespeherian Rag* by Terence Hawkes.

I have not yet come to the end of the shelf. Other shelves in this group carry similar varieties of books about Shakespeare. And there are two more sets of shelves in the hall and a bookcase in the small bedroom near the kitchen that carry Shakespeare books. I do not know how many "Lives" I have—Ivor Brown's, E. K. Chambers', Hesketh Pearson's, J. Middleton Murry's, Peter Levi's come to mind, and I probably have three books about Hamlet for every life of Shakespeare.

I am not as erudite as all this might lead a browser to think. Many of the books are beyond me. I am not a scholar. I built my Shakespeare library at random. I have no master plan. If a book about Shakespeare calls, I buy it. No other subject in this world interests me remotely as much as Shakespeare does. Any thoughtful view fetches me—feminist, Marxist, Freudian, cultural materialist. I belong to no camp except Will's.

Most of all I learn by reading Shakespeare. No matter how often I have read and seen a play, I seem to learn something every time I reread it or see it again; a line jumps out I have never before noticed, a bit of business changes my view.

I am corny about Shakespeare. As I write this, I wear an *Antony and Cleopatra* T-shirt from the Folger Shakespeare theater in Washington. I have more than thirty Shakespeare T-shirts and sweatshirts in New York and about a dozen on the island. It is one way I support the cause of Will.

A lovely porcelain statue of Shakespeare, given us by a friend, stands on a ledge in our dining room; borrowing from Keats, I think of Shakespeare as the presider. A small stoneware figure of Hamlet contemplating Yorick's skull sits on our piano in the living room; we bought it at Stratford-on-Avon in 1987. Betty and I were there for the birthday celebration four years ago today, seeing the flags of all nations unfurl from lampposts, the march of schoolboys and schoolgirls and official presences. Then anyone who felt like it joined the procession and dropped off a nosegay in the church. When we returned, a few hours later, the nave was blanketed with a fire of flowers from all over the world.

It was all touristy, I am sure, and I loved it because it was more than a memorial. Shakespeare had a show running that very night, as alive as ever. One of his capacities is to stride through centuries, so that he is not significantly dated. We saw *The Merchant of Venice,* starring Anthony Sher, who wrote and illustrated a compelling book, *The Year of the King,* about his researches into Richard III. Some of the people you meet in that book might keep you awake a moment or two, I will tell you that. You may not look so innocently at the middle-aged man walking his dog.

Shakespeare seems familiar to me. He is, as someone said, "a matey genius." I do not quote at length from the plays or sonnets. There were periods in my life, long ago, when I did not read him. But I grew up with him; he is always at my elbow. I've been acquainted with him about as long as I have with any breathing person.

I was raised in a middle-class, midwestern household. We were average, I guess, except that my parents were divorced, which was less common in those years than it is now. I later learned this meant that I grew up in a "broken home." I have been suspicious of jargon ever since. My home was complete to me. It is not bad to grow up the only male in a house with a mother and two older sisters who adore you.

Mother indulged me in a bad habit, allowing me to read at the dinner table. I suppose she thought I was better off with *The Ring* magazine and comic books than listening to chatter.

Still, I picked up useful information. My family read, and I heard talk about best-sellers like *Anthony Adverse* and *Gone with the Wind.* My sisters discussed beaus with our mother. They also discussed girlfriends, popular music, fashions, and Browning and Scott, Keats and Byron, and lots of Dickens and Conan Doyle.

My sister Anne, who was eight years older than I, read Shakespeare to me when I was seven or eight. I used to draw cartoons in a bratty kid brother manner, showing Anne reading a book labeled "Shakespeare," and I guess she wanted to prove to me she wasn't wasting her time.

She took me to see Max Reinhardt's *A Midsummer Night's Dream* when I was nine years old. Seats for the movie were reserved so you would know it was A Classic. I liked Mickey Rooney's Puck and Basil Rathbone's Oberon and the young women running around in see-through nighties, pretending to be fairies. (Betty and I saw the movie a half dozen years ago. Puck is usually a pain, and Rooney's mugging didn't help, but I still liked the girls in their nighties.)

After Anne died, her children sent me the little volumes of Shakespeare that had belonged to our grandmother, all the plays. They are in maroon bindings, and they are the worse for wear, but they are memory and I cherish them. Each is inscribed to grandmother from her friend, Miss Davidson.

Those little books were my introduction to Shakespeare. Not long ago, Betty and I had lunch with a woman who had been my girlfriend when I was fourteen or fifteen and she a year or two younger. She recalled that her parents told her they had liked to fall asleep listening to us read Shakespeare to each other.

People get a little crazy, thinking about Shakespeare. People at CBS, people at parties, people I do not know particularly well, people I have reason to believe do not spend their nights reading *Timon* ask me what do I think of the authorship question, that is, the idea that someone other than Shakespeare wrote Shakespeare. The current favorite is the Earl of Oxford, who enjoys the kind of support Bacon did a century ago.

I know that nothing will come of nothing, so I usually mumble and look for the nearest exit, an open window if necessary. The truth is, the authorship question does not much interest me. Shakespeare could return from the grave tomorrow and announce that he had been nothing but a poor player who lent his name to the genius lord, and I would think, Well, there's a good idea for "The CBS Evening News" and turn back to *Measure for Measure,* perhaps Isabella's "his glassy essence like an angry ape, plays such fantastic tricks before high heaven as makes the angels weep."

Why are people so interested in whether Shakespeare wrote Shakespeare? We don't know if Homer was a blind poet, a committee, or an oral tradition, yet Homer supposedly wrote every plot known to Western man. Only specialists care about Homer. People have given over lifetimes and fortunes to prove that someone other than Shakespeare wrote Shakespeare.

I am perfectly willing to accept the possibility that Shakespeare was a pen name, like Mark Twain or O. Henry. I am more interested in Hamlet and *Hamlet*. I cannot estimate the number of times I have read the play. My mother and sisters whispered Hamlet's name when they discussed Shakespeare. It was as though they were talking about cancer or Democrats. There was something mysterious, difficult, and possibly obscene about the play. I could hardly wait to read it.

I staggered through *Hamlet,* on my own, in high school and the navy. The light began to dawn in college, outside class. I not only read the play with notes, I read the André Gide translation in an extracurricular effort to learn French. That is one of my happy Shakespeare memories, drifting on a northern Minnesota lake in a war surplus life raft, a Schlitz cooling in the sea anchor, reading, "Etre ou ne pas être, telle est la question . . . "

I read *Hamlet* and reread it, and I read criticism of the play by the bookload, and I do not understand its hold on me, and I am not alone. A couple of years ago, I announced at dinner that I now knew enough about *Hamlet* to know I know virtually nothing about *Hamlet,* and Mike said, "Dad is beginning to talk Zen."

Had I the time I could become involved like that with other plays of Shakespeare and find plenty of literature to support me. Someone said each of Shakespeare's plays would repay a lifetime of study. I would not go quite so far, not quite.

A few years ago, we heard a brilliant talk about *King Lear.* The speaker was an eminent professor who had taught

Lear for years and had read it hundreds of times and had seen many, many productions. In an aside, she indicated her belief that Cordelia is alive at the end of the play. After her talk, I asked her if she really believed that or if I had misunderstood her. She said, "You mean as I stand here now? Yes, I believe Cordelia lives." She paused and added, "I may reread the scene tonight when I'm back in my hotel room, of course, and change my mind."

You do not read Shakespeare for certainties. Shakespeare is the voice of the establishment. Or he is subversive. He is dirty. He is boring. He is injurious to the morals of youth. Tolstoy hated Shakespeare. (Orwell said this was because Tolstoy was shocked to find he was Lear.) Shakespeare offended Voltaire.

More than any writer I know, Shakespeare has the capacity to cow people, make them doubt their senses. Leaving the theater, particularly Shakespeare in the Park, we hear someone say, "Well, I liked that. Of course, I don't know if it's Shakespeare."

Betty grabs my arm and pulls me away before I begin screaming at the stranger, "What *is* Shakespeare? Tell me that! Is it actors in tights and farthingales speaking lines with an English accent? Is it what your college professor told you? Is it some reviewer's opinion?"

I enjoy Shakespeare as I enjoy football. It is no more complicated than that. Shakespeare is considerably more difficult to understand than football and requires sustained attention of a kind few people seem capable of these days, but I approach the stage, as the arena, for entertainment.

Those of us born into a language close to Shakespeare's own may believe it is the power of his language which makes him Will. Our Great Poet. That language is certainly bewitching. It has entered speech so that we quote Shakespeare without knowing it—"vanished into thin air, high time, tongue-tied, more in sorrow than in anger, the devil incarnate, what the dickens"—the list stretches on. In Bartlett's *Familiar Quotations,* Shakespeare is quoted about twice as often as the Bible.

About one out of ten words in Shakespeare appears for the first time anywhere: *road, hurry, assassination, countless, obscene*—words as common as those.

But it is not so much the language, for poetry does not translate well, as the story that accounts for Shakespeare's international reputation. It is the story that powers Kozintsev's *King Lear,* Kurosawa's *Throne of Blood,* and Jean-Louis Barrault's *Hamlet.* The Russians claim Shakespeare. The Germans claim him. A Japanese professor recently said, "There is something about *Hamlet* that is very Japanese."

Dramatists praise Shakespeare's sense of structure. They teach playwrighting with it. The sense of structure is why Shakespeare may seem longer if it is cut. Mark Van Doren said *Hamlet* is its own synopsis; you cannot cut the play without hearing flesh tear. (It almost always is cut in production.)

About fifteen years ago, I felt my interest in Shakespeare slipping into obsession. I warned Betty. I said she did not have to accompany me; it could be like football, which she often ignores. She said she didn't think that would happen.

We have seen dozens and dozens of Shakespeare productions since then; she goes with me anywhere, storefronts and church balconies, attics, productions in New Jersey and Alabama and Connecticut and Minnesota, all three Stratfords. We go just about anywhere for Will. We were bride and groom when we attended our first New York Shakespeare Festival production in Central Park, and now Betty and I and the festival are coming up on thirty-five years together.

I am retired now, with more time for Shakespeare. That time could be given over to collectibles or playing the market. I am glad it belongs to Shakespeare, to Will and us.

Dispensation

Thursday, May 16

The walker Thoreau wrote, "No wealth can buy the requisite leisure, freedom and independence which are the capital in this profession. It comes only by the grace of God. It requires a direct dispensation from heaven to become a walker."

The dispensation touched me. I've been a walker all my life. I usually walked a couple of miles to and from Riverside High School in Milwaukee. I walked all over San Diego, San Francisco, and Boston when I was in the navy. I daily walked what I am told is five miles to and from the campus my first year at the University of Wisconsin.

As a young newspaperman, I walked all over Binghamton

and surrounding territory. I've walked in all seasons all over the island which is our summer home. I walked from my pad in Greenwich Village more than a mile to my job downtown, and I walked from our place on the Upper West Side to work at the *New York Times* building and at CBS.

My last dozen years at CBS I was torn between the need to read and the need to walk. My discretionary reading time was confined to my lunch hour and my bus ride to and from the office. Using that time wisely over the years, I had read *Remembrance of Things Past,* a dozen novels by Anthony Trollope, the seven-volume Dumas Malone biography of Thomas Jefferson, and I had reread all of Shakespeare.

In retirement, I should have plenty of time for both reading and walking. Exercise is urged upon people of my age, and walking is the only exercise I take that doesn't bore me. Walking is suitable for writers since it is possible to walk and ruminate at the same time. In fact, I find it almost impossible to walk and *not* ruminate.

Paul Theroux recently wrote of Graham Greene, dead at age eighty-six, that he "was unlike any other writer I have known in being physically fit without effort. When asked how he managed to stay in such good health, he said that he ate and drank whatever he liked and boasted . . . that he never exercised. In fact, he was an energetic walker all his life, but he loathed fresh air fiends. . . . "

I begin my day with a twenty-five-minute round-trip walk to Broadway to pick up my newspapers. I set out in mid-to-late afternoon after reading and writing and lunch, Aiwa in hand, and I listen to music as I walk for an hour, down an avenue, along side streets. I try to defy Thoreau who said, "Half our walk is retracing our steps." I try never to return exactly the way I went.

Even in retirement, I sometimes walk with a goal in mind. Recently, I walked about forty blocks to the Broadcast Center for a haircut and to chat with my former colleagues. The newsroom looks as though it has been hit by a neutron bomb. I am told that after a recent farewell party for a staffer, there were cake and ice cream left over. That was unheard of in my thirty years at CBS.

Because it is a collection of neighborhoods, New York is a small town. On another day, I walked fifty blocks back from a midtown office supply store where I picked up a couple of ink cartridges for my printer. I was listening to Italian pop on my Aiwa, and I must have been skipping for I became aware someone was watching me, and there at Eighth Avenue and Fifty-seventh Street stood Andy Rooney, who said, "You're having a good time, aren't you?"

On another day, business took me to Third Avenue and Fiftieth Street. I decided to walk back after the appointment, figuring the territory would be unfamiliar. I immediately passed a small hotel where Betty and I spent a wedding anniversary. A few blocks and I was at P. J. Clarke's, where the bar scenes for *The Lost Weekend* were filmed, and where I often ate lunch in the 1960s. I passed the site of another bar, now disappeared, which I thought was unbearably sophisticated. In the '50s, I brought young women there. A woman with blonde hair that was not a gift of God played a white piano. She wore elbow-length white gloves.

The walk in New York may surpass the event it leads to. Betty, Amy, Andrew, and I recently saw *Cirque du Soleil* in Battery Park. I liked the show, but I was delighted by the walk through Battery Park City, the nation's largest urban development project with three eye-catching office towers and apartments for forty-five thousand people. And the sun sparkling on the river before terrace cafes and no cars.

Walking is discouraged in much of the nation. Betty was stopped by the Beverly Hills police back in 1964 as she took an afternoon stroll. I came back to the hotel room and found her picking at a piece of fruit. "Johnny," she said, "do I look like a hooker?" She does not, but the fact she was walking near the hotel excited the police.

We spent last weekend at a motel in Gaithersburg, Maryland, where we visited Betty's mother in the nursing home.

We walked, with Betty's mother in her wheelchair, on a soft spring day. The next day, while Betty visited her mother, I stayed at the motel, read, and wrote.

I needed a walk. Highway traffic hummed outside the window. I took off my shoes, turned on a baseball game, and padded back and forth in the motel room, like a prisoner in a cell, fifteen steps each way. I did this for forty-five minutes.

In my retirement, Betty and I dance the Diet Dr Pepper ballet several times a week. This is our search of neighborhood groceries for my favorite drink. It is the only soda pop I know that stores are regularly out of. Either I am one of only two Diet Dr Pepper drinkers on the Upper West Side, or the drink is quietly, enormously popular. (A well-traveled woman once told me it tastes like the national drink of Yugoslavia.)

Diet Dr Pepper has replaced beer, wine, gin, vodka, and whiskey for me, and no other drink will do, so Betty and I dance our little dance past the familiar sights of the neighborhood, the beautiful schoolchildren, the bent old man on a stick, the woman with the dog.

Thoreau would not approve of this crowded city, but I know what he means when he says, "My vicinity affords many good walks and though for so many years I have walked almost every day and sometimes for several days together, I have not exhausted them. . . . Two or three hours walking will carry me to as strange a country as I expect ever to see."

Even in my unobservant state, I find a strange country in considerably less than two or three hours from my front door. The urban perspective, being full of people, changes more often than the countryside does. Only the buildings seem to hold still, and often enough they disappear and rise again, in a different shape and under new management.

One night last week, Betty and I walked a half dozen blocks to a friend's apartment, where a small group gathered to welcome Bob Simon, the CBS News correspondent who with three colleagues had been held prisoner by Iraq for forty days. One day he was told he was going to be killed as a spy. Back in his cell, Bob thought of Cavaradossi, awaiting execution in *Tosca*. Cavaradossi sings the aria, "E lucevan le stelle." Bob said singing about the starry skies was not what he contemplated.

On a chilly Saturday, I found myself walking around Shea Stadium, trying to keep warm as the dispirited Mets lost to the Pirates. I went to the game with Andrew and a friend of his. I always rush the baseball season. It is a long way to October, but I think the Mets are already plucking at the sheets.

Betty and I walked a few steps to a nearby building to attend a meeting of our newly formed block association. People unfamiliar with New York do not realize how strong a communal sense there may be here. We live in a building with a lively tenants' association, and we celebrate the building with lobby dinner parties.

I counted seventeen people at the block association meeting, five from our building. We are going to plant flowers and try to take some neighborhood children to a ball game. I hope to pitch in, although I will not be in the city for any summer activity.

❖ ❖ ❖ ❖ ❖

A recent headline from the front page of the *Times:* MEDICARE TO WEIGH COST AS FACTOR IN REIMBURSEMENT. Subheads explained: Fundamental U.S. Shift and New Rules say an "Explosion" of Expensive Technologies Requires the Change.

We recently received a letter from CBS, saying the company can no longer afford to pay the full cost of medical coverage. As of January 1, we will be required to contribute, the amount to be determined later.

The news is not a shock. For years now medical costs have climbed faster than expenses for any other basic need. Deep thinkers apply themselves to the problem but there is no solution I know of.

I forget about all this with a walk. The portable tape player may be the greatest of postwar inventions. I walk with my Aiwa hearing the ecstasy of Riccardo and Amelia, or hearing Sinatra sing for swinging lovers, or hearing Hamlet instruct the players, and it is, indeed, a benediction of retirement, to walk with no errand, obeying Thoreau.

Money

Saturday, May 18

"And now we come to that boring subject, money."

So said my sister Anne on an occasion many years ago, and she might have been speaking for her brother. Now people who say they don't care about money often care about it a great deal. No one but a blockhead or a saint is entirely careless of money and its uses.

But I think money leaves much to be desired as a topic. I was raised to believe that a gentleman never discussed personal money matters outside his home or office. I also was raised to hold a decent respect for a dollar honestly earned.

My mother believed the businessman was the most important figure in American life. Doctors, lawyers, and professors were all well and good, but it was the prudent businessman who kept the country moving. When I was a child, a rich and respected relative took me on his great lap, showed me a dollar bill, and said, "Now, Johnny. This should represent a certain amount of gold. But those fools in Washington. . . . " I forgot the rest of the economics lesson, but the phrase "fools in Washington" stayed with me.

My choice of trade, writing the news, indicated a lack of interest in making money. Professors urged me to a career in public relations or advertising, pointing out these would be more lucrative than writing about fires and office seekers. It did no good. I was newspapering's fool. When I started as a reporter, no one had heard of an anchorman, and newsgathering was a blue-collar trade.

I recall a Socialist newspaper columnist advising my journalism class that, if any of us planned on being reporters, we should remember we had more in common with the janitor than with the publisher. I didn't spend much of my working life hanging around with either janitors or publishers, but I never had trouble with the argument.

I had the newsman's mind-set of the period. You were doing well if you had a dime left in your pocket on pay day. If you had a dollar or two left over the chances were you would soon be voting Republican.

Betty was better trained than I to manage money. I marveled when I first met her because she actually kept an account book of her expenses. The thought appalled me. Any account book I kept would be a register of luxury and riot.

Not long after Betty and I were married, we reached some kind of contretemps about money. I had read that the chief cause of marital discord was, after sex, money. So I said to Betty, "Would you feel better if you took care of the finances?" She said she would and, to this day, she does.

(Betty's memory of this is different. She says she assumed control of the money after she returned from the island one summer to discover a stack of unpaid bills and checks written with no record of dates. I don't think this sounds even like me.)

For all these years, I have given Betty whatever I earned and I have taken what I need for expenses. This arrangement has worked so well for us that I am sure authorities would find things wrong with it, including sinister psychological revelations, but I don't know what would have become of us if I had had to deal with banks and financial forms.

When friends learned I was going to retire, they sometimes asked, "Can you afford it?" I answered that I could, although I only had a general sense this was so. I was determined to retire at age sixty-five, and I was not going to find some financial reason not to. It seemed to me that people who asked me if I could afford to retire had no intention of doing so themselves.

I did have a general idea I could afford to quit. Five or six years ago, Betty and I attended a preretirement seminar sponsored by CBS. Over the course of a couple of days, we heard from doctors, retirement authorities, and a man who knows about money.

The news at the seminar ranged from good (most of us present would still be present in ten years) to better (most of us, thanks to pensions and investment funds, would be all right financially) to best (sex goes on and on and on.)

I could have have retired then, but my pension would have been significantly less than if I stayed the course. And, in truth, I was not psychologically ready to quit.

After I retired, we hired a money management advisor. At his suggestion we took money from my Employee Investment Fund at CBS and rolled it over into various IRAs. We also live on the income Betty earns teaching and on money I am being paid to write this journal. Other jobs may turn up for me. We have excellent health insurance from CBS, for which we will be paying something as of next year. We have our summer place, which I inherited, and we live in a rent-controlled apartment we have occupied since 1961.

After the money manager ran our assets and expenses

through a computer he said, "Why don't the two of you take a trip around the world?" He was indulging in hyperbole.

The system has, so far, worked for us the way it should work. I think there is no more alarming drift in our economy than the threat to young people that they can no longer count on pensions or health plans, no longer count on a government that sees that employers live up to contracts. I don't think the business my mother revered and my gold-standard relative practiced have much to do with the business I read about today.

Old Friends

I don't know if it is because of the kind of work I did or because I live in New York or because it is a condition of life, but it seems to me that I lose touch with too many friends, people I like, people I think like me.

By retirement age, you are seeing friends die, or reading about the death of friends on the obituary page. Betty's best friend died four years ago, and not many days pass when Betty or I don't mention her. My newspaper mentors, Stu and Woodie, are dead. They seem forever thirty in my mind, but, then, "30" is the end of the story. Eli died. The other day I opened the *Times* and learned that the fellow who gave me my first job in television, and had to fight to do it, died out on the Coast.

There is not much to say about age and death without sounding like Justice Robert Shallow; "Jesu! Jesu! the mad days that I have spent!"

Now I am retired, I hope to catch up with old friends. In the past several days, I have caught up with two of them:

> Antonin Dvořák (1841–1904)
> Buddy, my friend from Village days

Dvořák is one of those great men who does not seem forbidding. He is an artist who inspires a feeling of closeness beyond the genius of his work. I suppose I felt this way about him from the first time I heard *From the New World Symphony,* and the feeling was even stronger after I recently read a meditation and a novel about him. Dvořák seems a Milwaukee kind of man; I can see him in a family tavern with a schooner of beer in the Milwaukee of the thirties.

Flipping through Saturday's *Newsday,* I found an item saying there would be a walking tour Sunday of the Stuyvesant Square neighborhood Dvořák lived in for a few years. It seemed an ideal event for a walker in the sunny climate of retirement.

Sunday was one of the ten most beautiful days since the world began. Betty and I decided to take her mother's car to the Dvořák walk. We were like the young immigrunts, thinking we could drive in the city on a gorgeous Sunday in the spring.

Half a block from our apartment, we encountered a parade down Central Park West. The newspapers the next day would say twenty-six thousand people marched against AIDS.

Betty turned into a side street. We faced a street fair at the end of the block. It was a broken field run just to get back home, two blocks away. We then did what sensible New Yorkers would have done in the first place; we took the subway.

We were walking along the northern end of Stuyvesant Square when two men stopped us. "Come to a beautiful concert in church," said one of them. "First we want to see the Dvořák house," Betty said.

The man pointed to Dvořák house, about a block away. He introduced himself and his companion, the singer William Warfield. We exchanged greetings, and Betty and I pressed on to join a group of some fifty people standing before the three-story Dvořák house while speakers denounced plans by Beth Israel Hospital to demolish the house and replace it with an AIDS hospice. The speakers said the proposed facility, with room for about a dozen AIDS patients, would not be adequate.

Our little walking tour, I realized, had us on a familiar battlefield: Progress versus history. What kind of progress? A few beds for a disease that needs a hundred thousand beds. What kind of history? A great man spends a few years in a house. Other forces were in the fray: all institutions, including hospitals, are guilty until proven innocent. The old camp follower, Not in My Backyard, may have been present, too.

Each of the antihospice speakers was careful to announce support for efforts to fight AIDS. The disease seems everywhere, marchers shuffling down Central Park West, speakers scuffling on Dvořák's stoop.

The concert in St. George's Church, which traces its history to 1752, included cakewalks and spirituals. Dvořák came to know Harry T. Burleigh, the first black member of the choir, and it is likely that Burleigh introduced Dvořák to spirituals. Dvořák later said, "The future music of this country must be founded on what are called the Negro spirituals," and he made use of them himself.

William Warfield sang. There were instrumental pieces. The choir sang "Going Home," an adaptation about which I have mixed feelings. The music left us shaky as we walked back into the sunshine, the trees quivering in the square, dark corners lit, even the basement stairwells splashed with light.

❖ ❖ ❖ ❖ ❖

Buddy and I met in Greenwich Village in 1955.

We lived in the same single-room-occupancy building on

MacDougall Street. At lunch yesterday, Buddy said those were among the happiest days of his life. I understood. We had been young in the Village in a kind of magical time, as Bohemia gave way to the Beats.

"Pad," "man," and "like" used as a comma were just becoming Villagespeak. The Village retained an aroma of its great flowering in World War I. A book editor I knew railed against the attorney general who got him kicked out of Harvard for subversive activities. The attorney general was A. Mitchell Palmer. The book editor ranted as though it had happened yesterday. You walked through the Village of the fifties with a sense you could drop in at Mabel Dodge's salon.

In 1955, Buddy and I regularly sat in a bar and told each other stories. He is a good storyteller and mimic. He was a painter, a Korean war veteran and a graduate of Hampton, doing graduate work at New York University and studying art privately. He told me about growing up in the projects in Atlantic City, about dumb white officers in Korea.

The routine back then was to bring a newspaper to the tavern and, over a grappa or a beer, dissect the United States. The Eisenhower administration offered plenty of targets for Village satirists although, of course, richer material was to come. The gents' room graffiti was largely a series of glosses on the scrawled statement "Kropotkin was the last of the true princes."

Buddy married his college sweetheart in the summer of 1956. I was an usher, a favor he returned later that year when Betty and I were married.

He moved to Brooklyn, then out to Long Island. He taught art in the public schools and moved into administration. Years went by when we didn't see each other. We exchanged Christmas cards and sometimes called each other and, on rare occasions, we saw each other.

In March of 1987, my union, the Writers Guild of America, East, went on strike against CBS and ABC. (Newswriters at NBC, who belonged to a different union, went on strike later, and it was even tougher.) We were a total of about five hundred writers, researchers, graphic artists, and desk assistants taking on two big networks.

The weather on the picket line was nasty. The strike lasted seven weeks, and it seemed as though it might last forever. I grew up in the 1930s, and I had read a lot about strikes and their economic consequences, but it is a shock for a wage earner to go from whatever he makes a week to zero. The strike was hardest on those who could least afford it, young people just getting started, often with new houses or new cars or new babies to pay for. But I never heard any of them talk about quitting. They were this tough:

CBS told us it was going to cut off our health benefits while we were on strike. (This is called "hardball" and is admired by unpleasant people.) On that dark day, in a slicing wind, we read that Thomas H. Wynman, the ousted chairman of CBS, was given $4.3 million to go away, plus $400,000 a year for life, plus lifetime health and insurance packages. All this, one newspaper commented, "for the kind of business performance that would lead a Japanese executive to commit hara-kiri."

I watched a group of young women read the CBS statement as they huddled on the picket line in the slanting rain. They laughed their lovely crystal laughter. The absurdity of it outweighed outrage.

It was a bleak time, the winds of March whistling off the Hudson a couple of blocks away under skies that seemed permanently pewter.

And then striding along came my old friend Buddy. I hadn't seen him in years. He smiled and grabbed a picket sign and joined the picket line. We marched along. He was working at the Museum of Modern Art, as a liaison with public schools, and he read about the strike and hustled over.

The strike, which never should have started, ended. The union came out of it with honor, and I don't know what else. It figured, when I thought of it, that Buddy would join me on the line.

I hadn't seen him again until yesterday when we had lunch at MOMA. We talked about our families, what's going on in the world, the invaluable small change of conversation when old friends get together. Except for Betty, I don't know anyone else who remembers the Village in the 1950s, the way it was, when things seemed within reach, Pollock at the Cedar Tavern, James Baldwin at the White Horse.

Harry Reasoner once wrote a piece about nostalgia in which he said that it is good we didn't know back then, whenever back then was, what lay ahead, or we wouldn't have been able to survive. As I talked to Buddy I thought how fortunate the two of us had been in our wives, our children, and our work. A hard part of what lay ahead for me were national experiences we would not have imagined in the cocoon of the 1950s, the assassinations of a president, a senator, a civil rights leader, the Vietnam War, AIDS. Who would have dreamed of such things?

A Weekend in the Country

Monday, May 27

The other day the *Times* ran a piece on the kind of dilemma it likes to help its readers solve. A couple buys a weekend place in the country and then cannot agree on how often to use it, one preferring a country weekend, the other the city. The *Times* favors compromise.

It is a problem Betty and I have never faced. Our country place is half a country away. When we go to Minnesota, we are agreed on the trip. We might have had difficulty with a weekend retreat. When we walk together in the city, Betty turns toward the park; I turn to one of the avenues, some vale of carbon monoxide with people and stores in it. We usually compromise and walk in the park.

When friends invited us to join them for a weekend in the country, my job complicated things. Country weekends start around lunch hour on Friday. My idea of leaving the office early was to get out at seven instead of seven-thirty.

Now I am a retired gent, and since Betty had no students Friday, this weekend of Memorial Day (Observed), we drove to the country Friday morning, to visit Lee at his place in the Berkshires.

One of the magical things about New York City is how quickly you are out of it. When I was a boy, I read that there were people living only a couple of hours from Times Square who had never seen an airplane. That may no longer be true, but sitting in Lee's living room, less than three hours from the city, we watched a sunset over the mountains that seemed a continent away from Times Square and, for that matter, the CBS newsroom.

It was a weekend of amused and ruminative conversation, much of it shop talk about a shop neither of us any longer inhabits. On Friday night, Lee and I watched "The CBS Evening News" together for the first time, although we had worked on the broadcast side by side or face to face for a dozen years. You do not watch the evening news while you are working as a writer or editor. You are on the phone, or writing or praying.

Late Saturday, Betty and I walked on a dirt road not far from the house. The woods grew right up to the edge of the road. There were many pines. Ferns stood waist-high and as fresh as spring. The thick woods grew dark.

We came upon a small graveyard in a clearing off the road, no more than a dozen graves or so. It was the cemetery you see in *Our Town*. Someone had thought to place flags at the headstones and markers of the Union dead. The dates on the gravestones showed the dead, as always, were boys— twenty-one years old, twenty-three years old.

That night we saw a story on the evening news about demands to return Memorial Day to May thirtieth because it is now moved around to make what only becomes a long weekend, and people forget the purpose of the day.

So it may seem to a politician in Washington or a television producer in New York, but when Betty and I drove home today through New England and New York State, we passed along flag-lined streets of small towns in their Sunday best to honor the dead.

A policeman stopped us in one town and told us we would have to pull over because the parade already had started down Main Street. Betty parked the car, and we got out and watched.

I hadn't seen a small-town parade in years. Here they came, out of days of the American past, first the veterans, not many and looking to carry about my load of years, not bothering to step too smartly; then the high school and junior high school bands. I am always surprised to see it is possible to blow a horn and simultaneously look self-conscious; the sound seems to contradict the image. Uniformed officers followed, then a couple of fire trucks, one of them a glittering 1990 purchase pointed to with pride, then Scout troops, and finally baseball teams grouped by age, some of the younger players not much bigger than the bats they carried.

We hear much talk about honoring the troops home from the Persian Gulf conflict, and that is fine. New York, which cannot find money to educate its children or keep its libraries open on weekends, plans a mammoth parade, paid for, we are assured, by private funds.

At the same time, I read that the Veterans Administration is cutting back on programs for the wounded of other wars. The VA wants to cut pensions for mentally disabled veterans. It also wants to eliminate its pittance for veterans' graves.

"We will always remember," we say about the dead of our wars. We always forget. We say we hate war, but we love parades. I started writing about Memorial Day in 1950. ("Damn it," the city editor growled, "your lead says they talked about peace and every damn quote in the story is about war.") I never found the right words for a Memorial Day story, but I never found anyone else who did, either.

I don't mean we should mark the day in sackcloth. The dead, being young, would not approve of that. But what seemed most right about this Memorial Day (Observed) was the little graveyard and the flags.

Lear

Monday, June 2

King Lear "anticipates much that our century has articulated: the callous cruelty of the human mind before Auschwitz and satellite newscasts; the wounding neuroses of the patriarchal family before Freud and feminism; the sanity of madness before expressionism, and the meaninglessness of life before existentialism."

So writes Lisa Henderson, de Barbieri Dramaturgical Fellow, in a program note for the Folger Shakespeare Theater production of the play, which Betty and I saw Saturday night. *Lear* certainly speaks to the last half of this abattoir of a century, particularly in our nation's capital, since one of the things the play is about is corrupt governors.

Lear recently has overwhelmed us. Betty and I saw Hal Holbrook as the king; we saw a gender-reversal *Lear* in which the patriarch is matriarch, her daughters sons, set in Georgia, USA; and Andrew and I saw a chair-throwing Lear in a company from Georgia in the USSR. We own videotapes of the Olivier *Lear* and the Peter Brook production starring Paul Scofield, *Lear* as *Endgame*.

Another thing *Lear* is about is adult children and an aged parent. (" 'How sharper than a serpent's tooth it is to have a thankless child,' " Mother used to say. She was kidding. So was I with our children. Laura once drew me a birthday card featuring "the hit song 'How Sharper Than a Serpent's Tooth.' " A woman in our building used to tell her daughter, " 'Oh, reason not the need!' " Her daughter would answer, " 'What shall Cordelia speak?' ") For all its grandeur there is something domestic about *Lear*.

This was cause for melancholy reflection as we drove down from New York. We made this trip four times a year for the past four or five years to take Betty's mother to the Folger. We would drive in early from Silver Spring and eat dinner on Capitol Hill, near the theater. It was a night on the town for Helen, rare since Russ died.

Now she is in the nursing home and cannot go to the theater. When we visit her, it takes too much time out of the weekend for us to drive to Washington from Gaithersburg where the home is, and so we decided we would end our subscription with *Lear*.

Helen has become a bedridden old lady. To those of us who love her, of course, she is much more. But that is her basic condition, and, in her words, it is hard to believe.

Until five or six years ago, Helen was independent. She is a woman from small-town Kansas who was the valedictorian of her high school and college classes, a Latin teacher who could design and sew a dress. She had lived in Greece and Nepal, and until not long before her illness, she studied Greek for the love of learning.

She had been driving a car since she was fourteen years old, in 1918, and she loved to drive. Well into her eighties, she drove every summer from Silver Spring to Minnesota and back and to and from New York at Thanksgiving and Christmas.

A few years after Russ died in 1971, Helen sold their home in Silver Spring and moved to a retirement community nearby. The quarters were smaller, but they were rich in the mementos of her life, artifacts and paintings, furniture and books.

Her decline followed a series of bouts with pneumonia. After one sickness, she fell in her bedroom, and she had to move to what is called "assisted living" at the Asbury Methodist Home in Gaithersburg. People there saw that she took her medicine and turned up for meals. It was when she moved there that she asked me, "What am I doing here, Johnny? It's hard to believe."

Betty managed to get her mother to the island through all but her most recent illness. She arranged for assistance at the airports, and she hired a young woman to stay in the cabin with her mother. She also got Helen to New York for Thanksgiving last year.

Then Helen had another bout with pneumonia. The doctor called Betty at night and asked if she wanted heroic measures taken. Betty said, "No." The doctor said, "Good. That's what I would have recommended." He wasn't sure Helen would live through the night. He was quite sure she would never leave the hospital, but he acknowledged, "These old people are tough."

That was a year and a half ago. Helen has been in bed or in a wheelchair ever since. The Wilson Health Center at Asbury, where she lives, seems to be a model of its kind. The help seems loving and efficient. It makes sense, under the circumstances, for her to be there. It is the best of a bad situation. That is the hell of it.

Betty calls her mother every day. She and Barbara try to get down to see Helen every month. Helen was a loving mother, and she receives that love and care from her daughters, but there are limits to what love can do, and this is hard on Betty and her sister. It is not easy for any of us.

Helen was an ideal mother-in-law, full of praise and non-interfering. Not long before Betty and I were married, we had a quarrel. It concerned a song lyric. Helen was present. Her daughter was clearly right. Helen didn't say a word. I never forgot that. Later, she often asked my opinion and told me I was a marvelous fellow.

She also was an ideal grandmother. Our children have had good breaks in their lives, but none was better than having Helen as a grandmother, just a short walk away, all summer long.

Now her face lights up the room when she sees Betty. Seeing her daughters, I think, is what Helen lives for. The other day, she asked Betty when she would be able to go to the Folger Shakespeare Theater with us again. Betty said, "When you get better, Mother."

Public Hearing

Tuesday, June 1

Retired people turn up at stockholders meetings, court trials, public hearings. They have all the time in the world.

Yesterday for the first time in my life, I attended a public meeting I wasn't paid to cover. The City Council Subcommittee on Landmarks was holding a hearing on the future of the Dvořák house. I was interested in the outcome of this clash between the past and the future. In this country, what we believe is the future usually wins. We are a land of tomorrow, impatient with history, perhaps the last people to believe in progress.

I approached City Hall by way of Nathan Hale's statue.

His last words stirred me when I heard them in Maryland Avenue elementary school. What would we think if he spoke them today, the noose around his neck? Who wrote his little speech for him? Has he no sense of *realpolitik*? Does he suffer from a martyr complex? This easy cynicism evaporated at the sight of City Hall, which dates back to 1812, and has survived decades of rascality.

The big room in which the hearing was held was perhaps a quarter filled when I arrived, with a dozen rows of folding chairs set up. By the time I left, in midafternoon, there was standing room only, and plenty of people were standing.

A daunting list of matters crowded the calendar we were handed, but I knew from hearings past that these are often dealt with quickly in order to treat the subject on the voters' mind.

I chatted with the fellow next to me. He was an architect, representing a Village restaurant which had applied for permission to open a sidewalk cafe. His real business, he explained, was designing prisons. He had worked on two new prisons for Riker's Island, a new prison for Staten Island and a remodeling of the brig at the old Brooklyn Navy Yard, to be used for civilians.

He said prison design is booming. We fill prisons faster than they can be built. His projections for the prison population were as alarming as the figures we shortly were to hear about AIDS—the prisoner and the patient may represent this society's two fastest-growing populations.

My conversationalist learned he was in the wrong room. He left. The meeting got started only forty minutes late. It began with testimony from two officials at Beth Israel Hospital. A hospital wants to open a place for the ill. Who could oppose that?

Plenty of people, as it turned out, whose basic argument was that the Dvořák building already was landmarked, that is, protected. This second hearing was needed to make the ruling permanent, but why the change of mind? Why tear down the sometime residence of a great man for a residence that will succor only a handful of sufferers in an epidemic?

Beth Israel insisted that the hospice was needed, and that this was the only site available. Beyond the specifics of the argument, I sensed a hostility toward the hospital. The pro-Dvořák, or antihospital, people asked about rumored plans to build a doctors' pavilion near the Dvořák house, about rumored designs on Stuyvesant High School, soon to be abandoned for new quarters, about rumored interest in a Salvation Army building up for sale.

The hospital denied any of those projects would be acted on soon, if ever, although the spokesman noted that any institution has to think of the future.

Each speaker was limited to two minutes. There were intelligent arguments on both sides. In a way, it was a case of the dead versus the dying. The matter was nowhere near settled when I left at three o'clock.

I thought this was an interesting debate, and I was disappointed to find no mention of it in the *Times* or *Newsday*. I called the Dvořák hotline this morning and was directed to the *Daily News*, where I found the story.

The meeting lasted until seven o'clock in the evening. The subcommittee said it will vote on the matter a week from today. Its members have much to think about, if they take the time.

❖ ❖ ❖ ❖ ❖

The Dvořák house was leveled. AIDS sweeps all before it.

Sudden Storm
Wednesday, June 5

A big storm in the country harrows us.

From calendar art to books to movies to experience, we share recognitions: the darkening summer sky, the lightning dance on the horizon, the rolling thunder, the first, spaced drops of rain quickening into a downpour, perhaps a lake turned black and snarling. The country thunderstorm awes us.

The same storm in the city is little more than a damned nuisance. In part this is the old prejudice that the green world is superior to the world of affairs. More practically, the rainstorm complicates city life, makes getting to and from work soggy and difficult, soaks the children and the dog, and turns streets into streams, washing out lunches and ball games.

The city storm also is high drama. I was reminded of this yesterday.

Retirement made it possible for me to join Betty, Andrew, and a friend of ours for the season's first free concert in Central Park. The performance doesn't start until eight, but space must be claimed at an hour when I was still writing lead-ins when I worked in an office.

The day had been hot and muggy. We have had a hot spell. It's been hot long enough to make people edgy. A couple of women vilified each other on the bus yesterday. It's the kind of heat that encourages drivers to beat the light by a second or two, sending pedestrians scurrying. It is mean heat that prompts bus drivers to pull away from the stop just as a late arrival, gasping and purple-faced, hammers on the side of the bus.

The weather people promised us late afternoon and evening thunderstorms, but they are wrong so often few pay attention to them. We nonetheless packed umbrellas along with deck chairs, a blanket, food, and drink.

We figured the weather might hold the crowd down, even though it was an all-Verdi concert starring Pavarotti. We did not set out until about an hour before the concert began. We found thousands and thousands and thousands of people in place when we arrived, other weather report agnostics.

We discovered a spot no more than a quarter of a mile from the band shell. The concertgoers were a good-natured New York crowd, old people, young people, lovers, children and babies, the weird. It was the New York crowd you never hear about, and why should you? Well-behaved people don't make news.

Now the sky darkened before dusk set in. The thousands and thousands of people companionably ignored each other. They ate, drank, and chattered, sitting on deck chairs or picnic blankets or newspapers. Smokers indulged in their vice without censure. A young man said to a young woman as they passed us, "They should put him on Valium." Balloons tied to posts bumped and clustered.

A Goodyear blimp drifted overhead. As night dropped in, the blimp floating above the trees and towers of the park was as dramatic as the ocean liner *Rex* looming out of the night in Fellini's *Amarcord*.

The speechmakers arrived. We could barely see them in the band shell, but their voices crackled over the loudspeakers, the mayor, then a representative of the chief corporate sponsor, then the parks commissioner, then the ever-present others.

And then, gathered in darkness, we heard Pavarotti sing arias from *Rigoletto* and *I Lombardi* and *La Traviata* and *Luisa Miller,* and then we heard the prelude to the third act of *Traviata,* the music filtered through loudspeakers and the murmur of thousands and thousands, and then we heard the pitter-patter of the first rain, just in time for the intermission.

The rain grew steady, the kind that gets under your collar. Then it poured. Balloons drifted off into the night sky. Mud oozed through the grass. Betty and I and our friend were on deck chairs, under umbrellas. Andrew was off jogging.

Lightning. Thunder moved closer. I asked Betty what she wanted to do. "Sit here," she said, "and wait for more music."

Only a few people departed. Some were with small children; some were without umbrellas. The rain fell like a waterfall off umbrellas. We settled in, thousands and thousands of us, like an army with no possibility of retreat. We heard resigned laughter through the rain.

To our right, a group that included small children stretched out under a plastic sheet. Before us, a young couple cuddled under a shared umbrella, nothing below their bodies as the earth turned to mud, so that if they moved a centimeter, they would lose the dry spot their posteriors created.

An announcement through the loudspeakers: "We are going to try to continue with the concert." Applause and, from a section to the front, the squeal of teenyboppers. The rain eased, but that was only a little joke.

Just as the orchestra struck up with the dark notes of *Macbeth,* the bottom dropped out of the sky and tons of water fell. It was time to abandon ship. People stood, scrambled, grabbed their artifacts. Betty under her umbrella laughed and marveled.

Another announcement: With apologies, the concert was off. There followed cheerful, insincere protests.

We headed out, slogging. The grass was mud. We reached a roadway in the park, where official vehicles parked with headlights searching the night, signifying nothing. Rain hammered on a line of Port-O-Sans. The crowd shuffled along, without complaint. By now, in the driving rain, umbrellas protected only the head and shoulders.

We emerged on Central Park West, the street to our left as we headed uptown. What we saw was as enthralling as any forest in a storm: a curtain of rain against the lighted windows of the towering apartment houses, the lights of cars creeping along the river that is often a speedway. To our right, the trees of the park were blackened and bowed by the rain.

Now the Pavarotti crowd vanished, into subways, cabs, buses, apartments, side streets, thin air. When we met other concert exiles, we exchanged damp smiles and thumbs-up.

Our air-conditioned apartment felt good. We left our soggy clothes in the hall. I took a shower, to wash the rain off. I heard rain snicking at the bathroom window.

I turned on the radio. A fellow with a cheery voice predicted continued heat and humidity with the possibility of scattered showers through the night.

Possibility? I hollered at the radio. *Scattered showers?* You must know, surely everyone must know, that there was a concert in Central Park tonight, Pavarotti, attended by thousands and thousands and thousands of people. There were other big events all over the city. There always are. Surely you know that, you dopes, I shouted. How did the rain affect those events? How about giving us some news on all-news radio instead of a weather report someone wrote at four o'clock this afternoon?

I was only hollering in my head. I had had too good a time to really be upset. I thought, I will see other great storms this summer, north woods epics; but only this storm was scored by Verdi.

Molly

Thursday, June 13

Betty and I are grandparents.

Mary Drake Horgan, who will be called Molly, was born at 11:52 last night at the New York University Medical Center. Mary and Molly seem to us lovely names, worthy of the beguiling creature we met this morning.

Laura called us with the news about 2:00 A.M. Betty and I had crawled exhausted into bed at midnight. Betty answered the phone on the second ring. I heard nothing until Betty called me to the phone.

Molly chose a dramatic time to arrive. After a sunny morning, the radio warned us to expect a series of potentially deadly lightning storms and, indeed, two people were killed by falling trees in the suburbs.

Laura said she sensed a change in her personal climate around the time the storm broke in late afternoon. At that moment, Betty and I were driving out of the city toward the New Jersey Shakespeare Festival production of *The Tempest*.

Betty had a hunch the baby might arrive yesterday. The baby—none of us knew the infant's sex before she was born—had been expected June first. Betty's feeling was no more than a hunch. Molly, like all babies, was the subject of great rounds of talk before she was born, and as the due date passed, there was ever more talk, so that Molly in effect was born with a history.

Betty, Andrew, and I went to the hospital the first thing this morning. It was a golden day, a duplicate of the June day on which Laura was born. Laura was just getting off the phone when we arrived. She did not look at all tired.

Matt brought Molly into the room. The first glance at the first grandchild. I broke every vow I had ever made about taking it all in stride, babies are born every day, do not over-react, etc. All the efforts of humanity, I thought, since we first emerged from the ooze and strove toward the sun, all the selections of all the mates through all the generations since the beginning of time aimed at the production of this one, perfect child. I kept this thought to myself.

I had to leave, after an hour of fawning. People on the street, the streets themselves, looked particularly splendid this morning. I reminded myself that my grandfatherhood would have limits. Those limits were established for me, forever, by a couple of weeks in 1964. I was writing a weekly football show called "Countdown to Kickoff" for CBS Sports. It was once cited by Russell Baker as an example of wretched excess, and it was great fun to write. We broadcast from a different NFL city each Saturday. We were winding up the season on the West Coast, rather than returning to New York—a week in San Francisco, a week in Los Angeles.

Betty had never been to the West Coast. Her parents volunteered to stay with our children for two weeks. Our four children ranged in age from one to seven. We also had City Girl, who required walking. Helen and Russ brought with them Helen's mother, who had just slipped into second childishness.

Betty and I enjoyed two carefee weeks, staying at the Beverly Hills Hotel in Los Angeles and the Fairmount in San Francisco, rolling around with funny people, seeking new heights of hedonism with our drinking and feeding, set to retreat, like Daisy and Tom, into our vast indifference.

Back in New York, our children for the only time in their lives fell simultaneously ill. Whatever they had involved sore throats, earaches, and fever. All the adults in the apartment came down with the plague.

Russ kept a log. It could serve as a warning to all grandfathers. It serves as a warning to at least one. Here are excerpts, beginning December 5:

— There has been no time to even pour a drink, much less to relax and enjoy it.

— Have wondered how Betty will manage when there are four children going to school on four separate time schedules. Just get a V.W. and keep driving, I guess.

— First time since our honeymoon I have seen Helen go to bed willingly by 10:00 P.M. Sick?

— Why should kids be given a toy containing of all things a bottle of ink?

— Don't ever buy orchids for the grandmother. Buy them for the gal who has the regular duty.

— Dec. 7. Helen's fever was 100.4 this A.M. My cold is about normal.

— Doctor looked at Andy Saturday P.M.

— Helen felt better immediately, after her fever backed down from 103. . . .

— Still no time for a relaxing drink. It was cool this morning, but Laura insisted she was warm in her red bathing suit. Stayed home with a slight fever.

— Monday. All in bed by 9 P.M. Colds and kids have done us in.

— Tuesday. No argument. Can't talk. Lost my voice.

— Thurs. A.M. The low point, we hope. Helen's fever of 104 is down to 101 and the ear drained. Mother B. had an accident in her bed, and we had an early morning clean-up to do. The maid is worth her weight in salt. . . . My voice is rough but hearable now. What a pest hole. Kids are o.k. now, though. . . .

— The low point turned into a depression. Helen's fever and earache continued all night. . . .

And so it went, or had gone, for two weeks. Temperatures dropped and then climbed again. There were "accidents" and vomiting. The doctor paid a house call—this was more than a quarter of a century ago—with penicillin and pills. Our cleaning woman volunteered to return on a Saturday. "That woman has wings," Russ wrote. By the end it was no longer clear who had a fever. Just "fever down ½ degree." By the end, too, Russ figured they would leave for Washington immediately on our return. "Helen can rest in a car seat better than here."

Betty, wearing not much, called our apartment in New York from our room in the Beverly Hills. I was sipping champagne and eating grapes. No sooner did Betty identify herself on the phone than I heard her say, "Tomorrow, Daddy. We'll be home tomorrow." It was the only time in our married life I heard Betty talk with either of her parents without being asked for an autobiography.

We flew back to New York the next day. We barely had time to set down our suitcases at the front door before Helen, Russ, and old Mrs. B. trampled us getting out of the apartment, running the storied Green Bay Packer power sweep.

A few weeks later, sports business took me to Washington. I visited Helen and Russ out in Silver Spring. He was in bed. His face was covered with cold sores, his voice a croak. That was when I set myself the limit of grandfatherly devotion I will not attempt to match. Laura told us a couple of weeks ago we would be sitting her baby for a couple of October weekends while she and Matt attended weddings in Florida and California. I said that would be fine as long as the baby, he or she, likes to watch football on television. I was practicing to be hard-boiled.

I don't know, though. Not after seeing that baby this morning. Perhaps because she took her time getting born, perhaps because I see her with my grandfather's eyes, Molly is an unusually beautiful baby. She weighed nine pounds, six ounces at birth, and her body is already firm, her arms rounded, her head perfectly shaped. She looks at the world with solemn blue eyes.

I am retired. I should have plenty of time to horse around with Molly. Laura and Matt live just twenty blocks away. I will have to work not to be intrusive. ("I just happened to be passing by, and I thought I'd drop in and see Miss Molly. Well, yes, I know it's two A.M., but I couldn't sleep, and I thought I'd take a little walk. What hailstorm?")

In today's sunshine, I thought of a song from a Broadway show called *New Girl in Town*. I used to croon it to our daughters when they were babies—"Look at her, look at her, excuse me while I look at her, and melt just like butter in the sun." I thought of E. B. White's verse, "Hold a baby to your ear / As you would a shell. . . . " I thought of Yeats's "A Prayer for My Daughter." That is a heavy burden for so frail a bark. How about *Mother Goose* and *Goodnight, Moon*?

Here I am, sixty-five years old, retired, and looking forward to being a baby-sitter.

Hooky

Saturday, June 29

One of my favorite New York stories, told years ago by an actor friend of our good friend Ray, is:

He came to New York in the 1950s, fresh from Northwestern, never before out of the Midwest. He found a room on Fourteenth Street, the northern outpost of Greenwich Village. A few evenings after he arrived, he grew hungry as he sat in his room reading *Ulysses*.

He ambled a few blocks up Sixth Avenue, book in hand, to a neighborhood deli. The counterman was a type the young actor already recognized: portly, stained white shirt, stubble, cigar butt in mouth.

The actor ordered a pastrami on rye. As the counterman busied himself with the sandwich, he asked the actor, "What do you have there?"

"A book," the actor said.

"I see it's a book. What's the name of the book?"

Pause, sigh.

"It's *Ulysses* by James Joyce."

The counterman removed the cigar from his mouth, a show of respect, and said, "*Ulysses,* very difficult. But I understand *Finnegans Wake* is the real ball-breaker."

It was at that moment, the actor said, that he realized he wasn't home anymore.

What that story says is one of the reasons why I never leave New York without regret. New York is unlike any other place I have ever seen. I've been thinking about this as Betty and I assemble things for our summer on the island in northern Minnesota. The island is the other place I love best. For me, this country comes down to a couple of islands. I think when most people say they love their country they really mean a few pieces of real estate.

I feel like a schoolboy with the three-month island summer given me by my retirement. Betty and I will stay on the island until she feels she has to return to her students, sometime in the early fall. Of all the anticipations of retirement, I think this promise of the island summer was most seductive.

But I know I will miss New York. I will miss family and friends, New York newspapers, "The CBS Evening News" and "Sunday Morning," some radio talkers found only here.

All of that is a small price to pay for our island summer. I also will be playing hooky from the city's problems—the poverty and drugs and homelessness. I used to think about this when we took the children to the island, and I witnessed their jump-up-and-down joy.

When our children were growing up, New York was not in as much trouble as it is now. But it wasn't old Milwaukee, either. I used to tell the children about the Milwaukee of my youth when I wanted them to understand that big cities can work. I was not able to give our children what I had growing up in the worst economic depression this country has ever seen: a sense of security on the streets, a belief that bad things will get better, a faith that government was on our side.

A thoughtful colleague gave me *The WPA Guide to Wisconsin,* published in 1940, as a retirement gift. Nothing has supplanted the WPA guides. This one validated my memory.

Milwaukee in 1940 was the nation's twelfth-largest city. It ranked ninth in manufacturing output. It always was in the top bracket of the thirteen largest cities in matters of health, safety, and solvency. (The mayor was a frugal Socialist, who served practically forever.) Milwaukee led the big cities in fire and crime prevention. The health of the populace was such that in 1937 Milwaukee was barred from competing for "the top health award" so that some other city would have a chance.

Milwaukee had the lowest murder and motor vehicle death rates of any American city with more than 250,000 people. The city won a national safety contest four straight years. In 1937, the city enjoyed the lowest per capita debt among the larger cities.

The WPA guide speaks of Milwaukee's reputation for "24-hour justice." It cited a report from a national crime commission which called Milwaukee "a city where a criminal is speedily detected, arrested, promptly tried and sent on his way to serve his time. No other city has such a record."

Not even Milwaukee is Milwaukee anymore. But once upon a time the city worked. New York worked pretty well, too, as I am reminded by my *WPA Guide to New York City.* Cities are in trouble these days. I cannot believe they are washed up.

I am playing hooky from urban concerns. Retirement has given me back my schoolboy's summer.

Road
Friday, July 5

Betty and I drove away from our apartment house Tuesday morning after Andy and Mike packed the car for us. A huge suitcase of clothes jams the trunk, along with two boxes of books, toiletries, and audio cassettes. On the back seat are smaller suitcases Betty and I will use on the trip, a suit carrier, Italian language and other tapes. My mighty Toshiba 1200XE is on the floor, along with my nifty Kodak Diconix 150 Plus.

I've never liked cars, even though I grew up with auto-mad midwestern youths. I thought cars looked funny, were too big for their job—hauling around a human or two—and stank. (I didn't know, of course, that the smell was deadly.)

Betty likes cars all right, but she and I shared stories about the misery of the Sunday afternoon drive, a feature of midwestern life in the thirties when the family would cram in the car for a spin, as it was called. Not even the balloon or ice cream at the end of the trip made up for the suffocating boredom. To be honest, Mother did not often enforce these improving journeys on me, and I trust that professional football, basketball, and baseball, being played on Sunday afternoons, have driven a stake through the heart of the enterprise.

But here I was in a car with Betty, set for a drive about half way across the country and in a state of bliss. Huck and Tom, Humbert and Lolita, Neal Cassady and his troop—I, the strolling figure these Odysseuses pass by, was excited to be on the road.

I had never traveled by car from New York to the island. I flew, the dullest form of transportation yet invented, useful only because it is convenient in cutting travel time for the wage earner with no holiday hours to waste, as I was for forty years. Betty had driven to the island a few times, always with children in the car, always pressing to get to the island as quickly as possible on the lullaby of the interstate.

Now we were determined to approach the island casually, following our noses through New York State and into Canada and down to Michigan and Wisconsin on the way. In spite of my aversion to cars, I love to drive with Betty. I provide commentary, jokes, appropriate silences. I change tapes. I hold the coins for toll booths. I watch Betty drive and marvel at it. I don't understand how anyone can drive a car. How can Betty keep her mind on what she is doing? If I had driven, I would have killed people, probably including me.

I was in high school when the poor fellow who taught my grandmother to drive when she was in her fifties tried to teach me. "Mrs. Mosedale," he told my mother after a scary moment with a bus, "this boy should not be driving." My attention span on the road has not improved, although I can watch the five acts of *Antony and Cleopatra* with full concentration.

And here was an example: Thinking those thoughts, I found we already were on the Palisades Parkway. I vaguely remembered gliding down West End Avenue and cutting over to the West Side Highway, hearing Steve Post predict, "Light rain for those of you on a diet," before turning us over to Haydn.

We stopped at a place called Lookout Point to check the Hudson, which appeared likely to be there when we return in the fall. We were in country fifteen minutes from the city, driving along Route 17 through southern New York State. We saw no signs of community.

The skies were heavy and gray, perfect for driving. Betty said, "No sun in the eyes." We were aiming for Binghamton, where I started as a reporter forty-one years ago and which Betty had never seen. Maybe the first newspaper is like a first love. In certain ways, you never get over it. It seems to me that all these four decades after leaving Binghamton, I have continued to try to write stories in a way that would please Mr. Cronk, the city editor.

How hard it was, and what fun. I wanted to be Stephen Crane or Hemingway, but I sweated over three paragraphs summing up what the day's speaker told the Lions, Rotary, the Kiwanis over aspic salad. The reporters I admired on the paper were more interested in writing, in how to write, and in books than anyone I would work with later.

My mentors. "Older guys." Probably in their early thirties then, and dead now, as if some jinx were at work. I see them still young in charcoal gray suits, the tilt of the head, the wave of the cigarette. I hear their laughter, their scorn at a political turn.

The rain hit as we reached Broome County. It came hard when we drove into Binghamton. The street names were familiar, but I didn't recognize anything. I mean, it looked like Binghamton in the rain, but I couldn't point and say, "There! In that place!"

We drove to Chenango Street, where the *Press* building is

located. The paper is out in the country now, and the building is office space. The bar across the street is gone, the hotel, the movie houses.

We ate in a coffee shop. I bought a copy of my old newspaper. It is no longer the *Binghamton Press* but the *Press & Sun Bulletin,* having gobbled up two rivals that kept us on our toes in my day, by God. Along the way, the *Binghamton Press* had become the *Evening Press,* inspiring a piece in *Editor and Publisher* called "Farewell the Masthead Roses." As I recall, the piece argued that if you found yourself in a strange city these days, you could not tell where you were by looking at the newspaper because place names have been dropped from mastheads, the better to convince suburban readers it is their newspaper.

Betty and I chatted over sandwiches and iced coffee. We were sharing this extraordinary feeling of freedom, but neither of us could say exactly from what it was we felt free. We were glancing over the newspaper, when in the sports section I found the obituary of a man named Frank Dolan.

Frank Dolan was the hunting and fishing writer when I was with the *Press.* He was enormously popular. The obituary reported he left the paper in the 1970s. He was eighty-nine when he died. The story was by John W. Fox, who joined the paper a little before I did and later became its sports editor.

I showed the story to Betty because there were names in it she knew. She said, "Why, Johnny, the viewing is going on right now."

"Oh, I don't think so," I said. "I'm not dressed for it."

Sometimes Betty knows what I want to do better than I do. I thought, Well, Frank was a good man who once introduced me to a fine young woman, and it would be a show of respect for me to stop by the funeral home.

Betty drove me there. John Fox was standing just inside the door. He looked as though he had seen a body rise from a demonstration casket, but he is a cool fellow and only said, "John Mosedale. What are you doing here?"

I said, "I came to Frank Dolan's viewing." Then I told

him what had happened. I said I had retired and was on my way to Minnesota to loaf and write a book.

"You're repeating yourself," he said. "Didn't you go to Minnesota to write a book forty years ago?"

"Close enough," I said. We talked a bit, then I signed the register and walked across the street and climbed in the car, and we drove away from the past.

We didn't get lost until we were near Rochester and couldn't find the New York State Thruway. That seemed preposterous, not to be able to find the Thruway, not even using a foolproof TripTik prepared by the Triple A.

Neither of us was irritated by this irritating turn. We were in no rush. Any minutes, or even hours, lost were not stolen from a small supply that would last only until I had to get back to an office.

"A quell' amor, quell' amor ch'e palpito," reflected Violetta on our tape deck.

"Amor e palpito dell'universo," Alfredo agreed.

We found the Thruway and arrived in Niagara Falls about eight o'clock as the sun poked through operatic clouds piled high over the water. The effect of the evening sun turned the falls into a chalk cliff and the rapids into gray moors. Fortunately, Betty and I were speechless. You are better off being speechless as you confront the falls or a sunset. The chances are minimal that anything you say will add to appreciation of the moment.

We took a room at Day's Inn. We shared the *Niagara Falls Gazette* at dinner. The great world trailed us. The newspaper reported that the New York State legislature continued wrangling over a budget long overdue; a Washington study found "teens lacking in job skills"; ten died fighting in Yugoslavia; vandals desecrated a Jewish cemetery in the town of Lewiston; a local black woman attacked President Bush in a column.

The *Gazette* carried word that the actress Lee Remick had died of cancer, age fifty-five. I interviewed her in 1957 when she was an unknown about to become known for her role in *A Face in the Crowd*. What an age to die; I thought back on the uncountable pleasures of the past ten years. I looked at a photo of a dead Yugoslav soldier. He was a boy; he probably was about the age of the Union dead in the little Massachusetts graveyard. How old were the dead in the Lewiston cemetery? Who would do such a crummy thing as vandalize their graves?

After dinner, Betty and I went to the falls for a nighttime look. The falls are illuminated for a few hours every night. The effect is hokey, as if someone were trying to bronze the water. I read that the falls have moved seven miles from their original location. Soon, as nature measures time, the falls will depart the Falls. What will become of the floodlights and the neon?

Young lovers sat on benches in the dark along the rapids, upstream from the lights. They were wrapped in each other, contemplating the foaming waters and the rapids' thunder, natural forces equal to the beat, beat, beat of their hearts.

❖ ❖ ❖ ❖ ❖

We were up at six. We ate the formerly healthful, now deadly breakfast of ham and eggs and strong coffee, lots of jam on the toast, perhaps real butter. We were on the road at nine. It takes us a while to get started because, as suspicious New Yorkers, we clear the car of valuables at night, bring the tape player, the computer and printer, my valuable papers to our room along with the suitcases. We must look as though we are setting up a money-laundering operation.

Betty and I appear innocent, however. Customs waves us into Canada. We drive through Hamilton by way of a dramatic causeway. I tell Betty the Hamilton newspaper used to give good play to my stories when I was at NANA more than thirty years ago; the long, self-absorbed memory of the writer.

We cruise around downtown Toronto, just sight-seeing. It looks clean and full of bustle on this sun-dappled day. I remember a story in the *Times* some years ago, a touring college professor who found Canadian cities so much cleaner than those in the States. I see no graffiti. We are in downtown traffic and no one honks a horn.

Ontario rolled by, woods and plains and outcroppings, a splendor of lakes as Fiordiligi, Dorabella, and Don Alfonso sang of soft winds and tranquil waves in *Così fan Tutti.*

Pushing west, we drove through sunbursts and cloudbursts, five minutes of sunshine, five minutes of heavy rain through the afternoon. The country grew a little more rugged, amber waves promising purple mountains while we laughed and talked. We worked with an Italian grammar tape, "E mio, E tuo, E suo . . . Egli mi vede, Egli ti vede, Egli lo vede . . . "

At the end of the day, a young woman in a tourist information booth at Blind River directed us to a small motel across the highway. We rented a room and dined in the motel restaurant. There were perhaps half a dozen tables. We ate whitefish fresh from Lake Huron. We were 896 miles from New York.

In the morning our breakfast included homemade jam as we looked into a countryside that was Eden. But the local weekly reported a search was on for a young fellow suspected of killing three people a few nights earlier at a nearby rest stop.

✣ ✣ ✣ ✣ ✣

Betty and I would make excellent terrorists, the round-faced, older fellow with the fair wife. Customs at Sault Ste. Marie welcomed us back into the United States with hardly a glance.

People at the Michigan restaurant where we ate lunch looked about twenty pounds heavier, on the average, than the Canadians we had just seen. Could this be? Wisconsin is supposed to have the heftiest citizens in the republic, but I do not think the citizenry in other midwestern states are notably slimmer. And yet it seems from the obituaries that no one in the north country dies before the age of eighty-five.

The rain fell as though we were back in Central Park with

Pavarotti. We drove through the upper peninsula, through Christmas tree country, in a downpour so steady we could not see the vehicle in front of us.

Then the sun burst through on a green and pleasant land, and I like to think that was because we were in Wisconsin, although I know that it rains there and gets bitterly cold and grows hotter than the engine room of an old ship in the South Pacific.

In Ashland we stopped to investigate an impressive white frame building with a cupola, clearly a Victorian relic. The clerk told us the hotel was built in 1985.

For the only night on our trip, for what we hoped would be the last time this summer, there was a place we had to be by the end of the day. We had to be in a motel room with a television set by nine o'clock, to see Bob Simon's report, "Back to Baghdad." We figure this will be the last time we will see television until late September.

We ate and checked into the motel and got a final dose of reality with Bob Simon's report and went to sleep in the north woods air. (North woods air, Mother said, starts at Brainerd, Minnesota.)

We awoke early. We had a final, unhealthy on-the-road breakfast. I will not knowingly eat another egg until we begin our drive back to New York.

In a couple of hours, a little after 9:30 A.M., we were at the boat dock from which we take off for the island. It was the first time either of us had arrived there in the morning. We looked at the island, green in the sunshine, two miles away over water that was improbably blue, as in a commercial for the Land of the Sky Blue Waters.

We had so much luggage to carry that we did not stop for groceries. We loaded the boat and took our luggage across. There are twenty-eight steps up the hill to our cabin. I counted them one brisk October day when my asthma kicked in.

There is not much to opening our cabin for the summer. We take down shutters and turn a thingamajig so that we can pump water and we unlock the outhouse. The cabin is a simple place. In an hour or so we were back on the mainland doing our grocery shopping. We hustled back to the island, as excited as children at the beginning of summer.

Retirement time, I thought. Retirement gave me the time for the lazy drive up here. This was Friday morning. We had traveled 1,552 miles since leaving New York Tuesday morning. I don't know if that is meandering or not, but I know that we would not have done it this way if I hadn't been retired.

Young people dream of retirement. Then as retirement gets closer, it seems to me that people become apprehensive about it. What will happen? What's it going to be like?

Just now it seemed fine. The sun hurt my eyes as it bounced off the lake. It was a clear day, just as it was that June morning sixty-one years ago when my mother, my sisters, and I first came to this place.

Sweet Sessions

Thursday, July 11

Mother was born and raised in Milwaukee. She was a child of privilege. I mention this only because, years later, her childhood friends could not understand what she saw in this little island, why she loved the island.

She met my father, a salesman, when she was at Vassar. After their marriage they lived in Toronto and Buffalo. My sisters were eight and six years older than I. When I was about four, my parents separated. Mother returned to her native midwest, to Iowa City, where her brother managed a store. She never talked about that decision later—she never criticized my father to me—but I think she went to Iowa City to make up her mind about my father.

Midwestern summers are brutal. They can be hotter than a baby's temper. Mother worried about her darlings in the Iowa heat. She worried about polio. We sweated through one Iowa City summer.

My uncle's wife was on the music faculty at the University of Iowa. She heard a psychology professor talk about an island in the north woods of Minnesota, far away from heat and polio. My aunt told Mother about this, and the professor put Mother in touch with a schoolteacher in Minneapolis, who was offering his cabin for rent. Mother took it, sight unseen.

I was five years old in 1930, too young to remember any of this, but my sister Anne was thirteen that first summer, and she remembered it well, and she told me:

We left Iowa City on a day of soggy, spirit-bending heat. The train windows were open so that air could circulate, along with the soot and the cinders. Mother was a little carsick. A gross woman climbed on the train along the way. She had just had her kidney stones removed, and she carried them in a jar, which she showed Mother. I was sitting in Mother's lap, whining for attention. I had been eating chocolate, which melted in my chubby hands. We sat up through the night and the next day. It must have been a nightmare for our mother.

We arrived in the late afternoon in the little town from which we would embark for the island. We were dirty and tired in our light summer clothes. Anne said it was about forty degrees, with a sharp breeze. The only person in sight was a man in a sheepskin jacket.

He directed us to a grocery, where Mother picked up food. A grocery truck carried us to the boat landing, and Mother hired a boat to take us to the unknown island.

There was no one around when we arrived. We were the first people on the west shore that summer. There was no electricity. Mother tried unsuccessfully to light the kerosene lamps. It grew dark, then black. In the helpful manner of children at a difficult time, my sisters and I began to complain and bawl. Mother made sandwiches, assured us that all would be well in the morning, and sent us to bed.

Not for the last time Mother was right. The next day dawned sunny and dazzling. It improved as the hours passed. We were for the first time in a land of pines, and we never recovered. Birds sang. The lake gleamed and beckoned.

The reason Mother could not light the lamps is that there was no kerosene in them. Our canny landlord rented us the cabin when he rented us the cabin. He provided lamps. If we wanted light from them, we bought the fuel.

The episode symbolized the inconvenience of island life. There were mice in the cabin. My first job was to empty the traps. (It is still one of my jobs, sixty years later.) There was no water in the cabin. We got our water from a common well, down a hill to lake level at the end of the bay. We loaded jugs, buckets, and bottles on a wheelbarrow, filled them, and returned to the cabin. There was no ice box in that cabin. Food was cooled by placing it in a cement-lined hole in the ground. This assured that the milk was always sour, which made me ill.

Mice were the only thing I ever saw my mother fear, and mice aside, Mother loved everything about the island. It was mysterious. Grandmother visited just once. Ever after she said, "I don't know what Harriet sees in that place where you have to grope around in the dark."

There are no stores on the island. In the 1930s, people on the west shore didn't go to the mainland often. Some of us didn't even own boats. We all ordered groceries through the mailman. A grocery boat brought supplies three times a week, so there could be a wait for something you needed, unless a neighbor had it.

A mailman delivered mail by boat six days a week. This practice lasted through the Great Depression, the biggest war in the history of the world, the cold war, and its aftermath, through administrations Democratic and Republican, until the Bush administration.

We used in 1930, and still use, an outhouse. This did not

trouble Mother, who was at least as fastidious as some people I have heard express horror at the idea of a privy.

Just about everything about the island was inconvenient. Mother loved it. No wonder her friends were baffled. Mother was in no way an outdoorswoman. She did not fish, sail, or canoe. She didn't even swim. Once on the island, her goal was to not leave it. I doubt that she averaged more than three trips to the mainland a summer.

My sisters and I loved the island, too, but we were children, and it would be an unusual child who didn't like island life. We were free to romp in the woods, dash over island trails, and jump and splash in the lake. In that cabin there was a bed made of birch logs and suspended from the ceiling. Early one morning my sisters and I watched as a moose swam from the island to the mainland, its great head and antlers black against the early sun. It remains the only moose I have ever seen up there.

The next couple of summers, Mother rented another cabin. This new one was magical. The owner, a bachelor from across the lake, had papered the walls with magazine covers. Covers of old *Colliers* and *Saturday Evening Posts* and *Americans*, covers showing dogs and cats playing cards, monkeys doing crazy things, a lovely maiden against a crescent moon. How dazzled I was! I begged Mother, begged her, to fix up our apartment in Milwaukee like that. But she would no more hear of it than she would buy me the tommy gun I wanted for several Christmases.

In 1934, Mother rented the cabin that is now ours. She bought it two years later. She named it—cabins had names in those days—Granli, which supposedly means "pine-covered island" in Norwegian, although I have not investigated. In 1940, she had a well dug, the first private well on our shore. The diggers had to go more than 130 feet deep, but they hit water we find surpassing. She then built a room around the well, which is where we eat in the summer. It is called "The Pump Room," after a celebrity hangout in Chicago.

The 1940 well is the last improvement that's been made

on the cabin except for a small bedroom Mother had built for me as I lurched into my teens. Electricity came to the island in 1952. Although Betty and I did not know each other then, we both denounced electricity's arrival. This is because, as we were to learn from our children, the young are natural Tories who do not want to see any change for fear all will change.

"The summer place" is an evocative phrase. For people lucky enough to have known a summer place from infancy, the words summon up family, friends, lovers, childhood. Guests may praise the island, perhaps politely, but they do not share the memory of the long summers of the depression when people on this shore arrived in June and stayed through Labor Day and the sun baked the water so that even the spring-fed lake turned tepid.

No one had money in the depression, so we stayed put on the island. There is more money now, and most of us grab what time we can take, two weeks or three for most men. Only the ignorant believe money can buy everything.

In memory, the America of the thirties was monochromatic. Against that backdrop, Granli was a bright splash of color. I remember falling asleep to the sound of parties in our cabin, college and high school men and women laughing. They danced to the wind-up phonograph playing songs like "The Lamp Is Low" and "Gone with the Wind."

My sisters were in their teens, and I grew used to sudden storms and sudden calms. Then my sister Anne was writing her fiancé's name in the air, or on pieces of paper she left lying around the cabin, given name and surname, name with middle initial, name with two initials, name with "Mrs." in front of it. A string of suitors attended my other sister, Dote, young men with midwestern or southern or eastern or sunny California accents.

I thought my interests at the time centered on sports, games the family lumped under the generic title Disaster, and reading *The Shadow* and *Doc Savage*, but of course I wandered into the climate of romance, and as if by osmosis, I absorbed the conviction that things will turn out beautifully.

I grew up believing in the promised kiss of springtime that makes the lonely winter seem long, that when it's springtime in the Rockies, I'll be coming back to you, and that you'll embrace me, you sweet embraceable you. (Even the blues of those days were likely to be a torch song, in itself a tribute to fidelity with its insistence that the only person in the world you could possibly love doesn't love you back.)

When I was in eighth grade, my mother bought me a rowboat and a secondhand, three-quarter-horsepower outboard of the sort fishermen used for trolling. This was my boat and motor until I went into the navy.

I became insane about a girl when I was fourteen years old. The three-quarter-horsepower Evinrude Elto was speedy enough to carry me to her and us to wherever we were headed. That is what convinced me I would never be in a hurry on the island.

Mother said that before any of us married, we should bring our intended to the island. She meant you will get a good idea of what someone is like by living in close quarters with them, away from city distractions such as movies or a night on the town.

Anne married an islander. My first girl was an islander. Three days before I went into the navy, I met a young woman on the island. In boot camp, at Great Lakes, my barracks was next to the highway which was just outside the fence. I thought of her in the summer night, above the sounds of 120 men breathing and snoring and groaning, when I heard girls' laughter from the roadhouse where the juke box played "I'll Walk Alone" across the whispering highway.

Once on the ship when I didn't hear from her at mail call, I kicked a steel cabinet door off its hinges.

That girl and I broke up after the war. I came to New York and found everything I thought I needed. Then I met Betty, already an islander, and so found all I had been missing.

One way I know I have matured is this: Betty and I have lived through long, painful summer separations. She and the children spent the summer on the island. I got up there for two or three weeks, whatever time I could take. Betty and I wrote each other every day. When the post office nodded, and I didn't get a letter from her, I no longer kicked inanimate objects, although I often felt like it.

When the children were little, they wanted to do everything at once on the day we arrived on the island. They were overexcited, wanting to swim, hike, visit. Joy paralyzed them into a kind of insane obedience. "What cán we do? What can we do?" they cried. I would say, "Run around the cabin ten and a half times," and they would do it. Or I would say, "Run into the next bay and back three times," and they would do it.

Love for a summer place, like any other kind of love, makes the lover crazy. I have heard a perfectly respectable, law-abiding citizen say, "If anyone tried to change this island, I believe I would kill him."

Thinking of the island summons up sweet sessions of silent thought, and each day adds to the store. Island Fourth of Julys march through my head. In my lawless youth, firecrackers marked the day, from ladyfingers, which were harmless and kid stuff, to cherry bombs, a bigger bang, destructive and thus adult. I deafened myself for a few days after I dove the wrong way when a cherry bomb exploded. Firecrackers have pretty well passed from the west shore scene, I am happy to report, but the communal picnic endures.

The picnic used to be held in the yard between our cabin and a neighbor's. One Fourth it poured. The grown-ups decided to hold the picnic on our screen porch and our neighbor's, dividing the picnic up. There was much discussion among the adults. I later learned the talk was about who would be on the porch where the kids were.

The picnic this year was held in a yard a few cabins away, on Saturday the sixth so that weekend islanders would have a chance to join. It was a sunny occasion. Among those present were grandchildren of people I knew as children. The new children were energetic and well-behaved.

Betty and I have already canoed to the sunset a couple of times. Well, not quite, but we know now just where the sun dips into the lake, and one of these evenings we'll be there in time to capture it.

We have dined out once since we arrived and entertained company twice. We haven't done much walking yet. We had to make one trip to the mainland, for groceries. It is cool for July.

Islanders do not ask me how I am enjoying my retirement. Instead, they say, "Isn't it wonderful you are retired. Now you can spend all the time you want up here."

Bastille Day
Sunday, July 14

Betty and I spent a quiet Bastille Day.

In fact, I did not notice the date until this evening. It has been years since I have been on the island on July fourteenth, and I have gotten out of the habit, but Bastille Day used to be celebrated in this cabin.

I suppose Mother was the last family member to have read Carlyle, and my sisters and I saw the French Revolution through the eyes of Dickens. I understand historians are now saying the French Revolution wasn't really necessary; I'm told some historians say the same thing about the American Revolution. Historians change their minds more often than scientists do.

One year when I was in high school, my sister Dote and a friend and I were chugging back to the island from the mainland. Dote's husband had gone overseas not long before, and she was jumpy, smoking a lot, tapping her foot. Now she turned her pretty face to the sun and muttered, "There must be some reason for a party today." She turned to us. "It's Bastille Day!" she said.

We threw a little party at our cabin that afternoon. I brought my girl. We rounded up what young people we could find. We danced and drank Coke and beer. The celebration, born of wartime, continued fitfully in peace, until Betty and I revived it, carrying wine through the woods and offering a glass to anyone wishing to toast the French on their holiday. The only recording we own of "Le Marseillaise" is by the Mormon Tabernacle Choir, and I search for something more, well, revolutionary.

One of my favorite Bastille Day observances occurred last summer when we were in New York. Betty, her mother, Andrew, and I were invited to Lee's. We entered his apartment to the sounds of Piaf and Montand. A fine meal followed, worthy of the French, topped by evil pastries. Then Lee turned on his VCR. Up came the great scene from *Casablanca* where, at a nod from Humphrey/Rick, the band and his clients break into "Le Marseillaise," drowning out the German soldiers and their anthem.

The movie, like our first island celebration of the day, came at a time when this country entertained warm feelings toward the French, some memory of the ties between the two great republics, perhaps the recognition that without French men, materiel, and money we would not have achieved our independence when we did. The French can be difficult to take, but what people can't be?

There is a good deal of French-bashing in this country these days. It has become fashionable, like Japanese-bashing. I guess all countries bash other countries; it is a way for the basher to avoid responsibility for his own shortcomings.

Perhaps by our next Bastille Day we will have learned how to build a high-speed train from the French and how to establish a day-care system. In the meantime, I will seek a really rousing "Marseillaise."

Old News

Friday, July 19

"Three-quarters of news is new." "Nothing duller than last week's newspaper."

Unlike most clichés, those are not true. Old newspapers, old magazines, old letters give us the truest sense of what yesterday was. In a storage space in the bedstead Andy carpentered for Betty and me, there are boxes of magazines— *The New Yorker, The Ring*—and boxes labeled "J's Papers & Letters," subdivided into "High School & College," "Navy," "Binghamton," and the like. I think Mother saved everything I ever wrote. It is a family habit. I have saved all of Betty's letters and letters from our children.

"Someday I'll take a look at that stuff," I have told myself for years. In this first summer of retirement, I will have time. I will be a cartoon figure: Retired Guy cleans out attic, closet, garage, tries on old service uniform, finds old love letters, finds . . .

What I found today was *The New Republic*, a box of the magazines I assiduously read in the 1960s and '70s. I was attracted by an issue published just twenty years ago—the issue for July 24 and 31, 1971. Its cover promoted an article, "Gun Toting" by TRB, the column then written by the elegant Richard Strout of the *Christian Science Monitor*.

The column begins with an account of a late-night visit by reporters to the suburban home of Chief Justice Warren Burger. He answered the door in bathrobe and pajamas, toting a long-barreled revolver.

TRB wrote, "The Chief Justice of the United State Supreme Court answering his doorbell with a gun somehow typifies the law-and-order issue in America today." TRB found the national obsession with guns "the one thing in barbaric America that even the most tolerant and sympathetic visitors from civilized countries outside cannot understand."

He quoted Milton Eisenhower: "There are at least 25 million handguns, perhaps 30 million in the U.S."

Twenty years ago. Earlier this year, I cut out a paragraph from a Jimmy Breslin column: "From 1985 to 1989, the number of guns in this country grew by 12 percent. There are now 200 million handguns, rifles and shotguns in the United States. In addition, the country imported another 18 million guns. That means in those four years, the number of new guns in this country was more than the number of births."

My eye fell on another *New Republic* cover, this one touting "No More Nonsense About Ghetto Education" by Joseph Alsop, the establishment Republican columnist. He argued that desegregation is the ideal, but that in the meantime billions of dollars must be invested in black schools. He conceded, "The outlays for adequate reform will be enormous, indeed . . . to insure quality education in ghetto schools that are beyond practical reach of early desegregation."

The date of that article was July 21, 1967.

"Maddox of Georgia," "SDS Convention," "Svetlana"—many of *The New Republic* articles are history. But the most dated fact of all is how I got the magazines on the island. They were forwarded by a postal clerk, the summer address written by human hand, additional postage seven cents.

A Woman's Eyes

Monday, July 22

Our human vulnerability does not disappear in retirement, not even on the island. We always are healthy on sufferance. A germ or an accident fells us randomly as the breeze touches our face, blown from nowhere.

Following a brisk afternoon rain a week or so after we arrived, Betty and I headed for our daily swim. She was on the front stoop, a few steps ahead of me as usual, when I entered our bedroom to change.

I heard her call my name in a small voice. I didn't hear what she said next. I stepped to the porch to ask her what she needed.

She was seated, like a little girl playing in the sand, at the foot of the three steps from our front stoop. She wore a terrycloth robe and a bathing suit. Her towel, soap, shampoo, and hairbrush were strewn across the path.

"I've had a fall," she said quietly. "Watch yourself on those steps." The steps were slick from the rain. Betty said she felt faint. She stayed put. After a time, I led her to the little screened porch, where she lay down. I fixed her a cup of hot tea.

Less than an hour later, we were swimming, horsing around with a neighbor boy, laughing. Betty cooked dinner for the two of us. We walked to the next bay so that she could call her mother.

When we returned to our cabin, we read for about an hour. Betty was lying on the sofa with a shopgirl novel in Italian. At bedtime, she said, "Johnny, I can't get up."

I thought she was joking until I looked at her. I offered her my hand. She gave an odd, disembodied laugh. "It's the strangest thing," she said. "I can't get up."

I helped her to her feet. She laughed again, then began to cry. "I feel sort of hysterical," she said. "I'm freezing." Her hands felt as though she had come in from a January night.

I got her to bed, turned on the electric blanket, and boiled her a cup of hot water. She worried about her right hand, which she could not open without pain. The next morning, though, she seemed fine. Her fall was forgotten, except that I couldn't shake the image of her sitting at the foot of the steps.

It was almost painfully sunny today. In the afternoon, Betty and I walked in the woods. We found a spot we love. We sat near the lake. Betty said, "Johnny, I want to tell you something."

I know that tone. It is never good news.

She said she had been picking raspberries the other day when a fat, black blur flashed across her left eye. She had been seeing floaters in that eye for some time. She went to an eye doctor just before we left New York, and he told her floaters sometimes occur as people age, and sometimes the floaters go away and sometimes they don't. He said she should only be concerned by a dramatic change in the size or shape of the floaters. Then, he said, she should see an eye doctor right away.

Betty said she didn't know if the changes warranted a call to the doctor. We both knew what she should do, but I knew how she felt. We are having such a good time we do not want it interrupted by problems. We want to do, more or less, nothing, which is the toughest of all summer dreams to make come true.

We talked with a neighbor who is a doctor. He suggested Betty call her eye doctor in New York. That doctor was out, but she will try again tomorrow.

❖ ❖ ❖ ❖ ❖

Tuesday, July 23

Betty and Mike were going to town today to run some errands. I was going to stay on the island with Amy and her dogs. Betty and Mike went to the next bay to fetch the boat after Betty called her eye doctor in New York.

A little later, the boat pulled up to our dock and Betty called to me and said the eye doctor in New York told her to get to an ophthalmologist right away.

We believe in what might be called "islandness." It shields us from the realities of the harsh world across the lake. It is a faith which is often shaken, but we are true believers, dismissing evidence and logic. Leave the island to see a doctor?

People die on the island, fall victim to many of the diseases of humankind, get drunk, smoke pot, who knows what else, get mumps (me, age ten), step on nails (Laura, very young), fall from trees (Michael, very young), suffer from an impacted wisdom tooth (Betty as a young mother, and an electrical storm knocked out power midway through the extraction, so the dentist finished with sledgehammer and crowbar), catch colds (Mother said this only followed visits to the mainland, or contacts with people who recently had been to the mainland, where germs lurked), pick up sunburn, swimmer's itch, poison ivy, and hay fever, rashes of fly and mosquito and spider bites, endure attacks from wood and deer ticks and, of course, people drown in the lake.

In spite of all, we believe that islandness prevents us from getting sick.

Mike drove us across the lake and then to the clinic about twenty miles away. Fifteen or more patients were waiting when we arrived. The clinic is a clean, well-lighted place, and the receptionists were polite and efficient. Before long, a doctor summoned Betty. She responded, clutching her novel, *La Carta Vincenta*. I heard her ask plaintively, "Is it all right if I read?"

The doctor called us in. He said he had discovered a tear in the retina of Betty's left eye. It was too big to be treated at the clinic; she would have to go to Minneapolis immediately. He would make the arrangements. He said the fall *might* have caused the tear.

Betty, Mike, and I ate lunch in town while the arrangements were being made. None of us spoke of our worry. We talked about how we could hold time away from the island to a minimum. We laughed a lot. When we returned to the clinic, we were told Betty's appointment to see the specialist in Minneapolis was set for tomorrow morning. We decided to drive down to the city tonight.

Back at the island, we swam, visited friends, ate dinner. We hoped the doctor would treat Betty in the office tomorrow, so that we could get back to the island right away. This was a realistic possibility.

If I still worked in an office, I would have left the island for New York last Sunday. I would now be flying to Minneapolis, or Betty would be flying to New York.

We left the island a little after seven in brilliant sunshine. I cannot count the number of times I have traveled the two-hundred-plus miles between the island and Minneapolis, by car, by bus, by train, by air. But none of us had ever made the trip for a medical emergency. We had brought along tapes, but we spent the time in talk and silence. We didn't discuss

Betty's eye. We weren't avoiding the topic. There was not much to say.

❖ ❖ ❖ ❖ ❖

Wednesday, July 24

We slept last night in the home of friends. The last time Betty and I were here, six years ago, was the day after a daughter of the house married. It was a happy time.

There is nothing quite so dark as an unfamiliar house in the night.

Betty had been told not to eat breakfast before seeing the doctor. I suggested she stay in the house while Mike and I ate out, but she came with us. The breakfast newspapers carried accounts of a singularly disgusting series of murders in Milwaukee, the oasis of my childhood.

Why do I feel guilty when Betty or one of the children is ill? When we were first married, I grew so angry when Betty got sick that she thought I was sore at her. I am better about this since I heard a grandmother at an AA meeting say that only when she put aside the bottle did she realize that she was not responsible for every illness or black mood suffered by her children. It may be that one of alcohol's illusions is that the drinker can control everything.

At the hospital, Mike and I were summoned not long after an aide led Betty to a doctor. We watched the doctor examine Betty's eye. He confirmed that she had suffered a tear of the retina. There was some detaching. Surgery was needed. He said that while the tear was big, it was not easy to find, and he commended the north woods doctor for discovering it. He talked to Betty's doctor in New York, describing the tear as "at twelve o'clock, above the horizon."

Then, taking his time, he explained the operation to us in standard American English. He invited questions. He said that he would put a buckle on the site of the tear, a small piece of plastic, and place a belt around the eyeball to hold the buckle in place. This wonder is apparently routine.

The doctor could not find space in the hospital to operate tonight. The operation is set for 10:45 tomorrow morning. Betty can eat until nine o'clock tonight. We drove to a supermarket and picked up food. Mike left us to visit friends.

Earlier in the day, with time to fill, this family did what it often does with free time, particularly in crisis. We visited a bookstore. Betty bought *September,* a novel being admired on the island. I bought *If No News, Send Rumors,* a collection of journalistic sin and error.

But tonight as we sat reading in our comfortable, borrowed living room, Betty yelped. She was looking at pamphlets the doctor had given her. "Johnny," she cried. "It says here I can't read for a week after surgery."

The pamphlet also said, "Even though the surgery for retinal detachment is generally successful, certain complications can occur. Any of these complications can result in failure of the operation, loss of some or all vision, even the loss of an eye."

The loss of an eye! It is a terrible thing to contemplate. I looked across the room at Betty, who was sitting in soft shadows.

It is the woman's eyes that fetch men. I thought of high school friends, shipmates, college fellows, men I've known all through my life. They might be coarse about women—I'm a leg man, an ass man—but when they met their destiny it was the eyes they spoke of. You never saw such eyes. They were incomparably brown, blue beyond compare, green eyes of immeasurable depth, hazel eyes . . .

Betty and I went to bed. I looked into her eyes and kissed her good night and turned off the light.

❖ ❖ ❖ ❖ ❖

Thursday, July 25

After they took Betty away from the reception area at the hospital this morning, the last thing I heard her say, her voice trailing off, was "When will I be able to read?"

Mike and I were told we would not see the doctor for at

least two hours. We left and ate breakfast. Then we stopped at a K-Mart, where I bought Betty a tape player. Then we went to a bookstore and bought Betty a Garrison Keillor tape, and I bought a book for an island friend's birthday, and I bought myself a reissue of the 1938 *WPA Guide to Minnesota.*

Back at the hospital, waiting, I reminded myself that I was not responsible for the fact that a doctor was sticking a knife or something like a knife in or around my wife's eye. Each year, I reminded myself of being told, about one out of every ten thousand people in the United States suffers a detached retina.

A little after noon, a yellow-jacketed volunteer led Mike and me to a waiting room. The doctor appeared, still in surgical gear. He was on his way to another operation, but he stopped to talk with us. He said the operation had gone well. I am sure we repeated questions we had asked him yesterday, but he took the time to answer them.

About two o'clock, Mike and I saw Betty. Both her eyes were patched. The doctor had explained why this was done, but I forgot the reason. Betty smiled and waved feebly at us. She was nauseated as an aftereffect of the anesthesia. She didn't want to talk. The doctor had said she should sleep as much as she could.

Betty was in a double room, and her roommate, hidden by a curtain, was watching television. I thought, guiltily, how Betty hates most television.

I sat on a chair in the hall outside the door to her room, reading my WPA guide. I sat in a hospital in Minneapolis, reading about Minneapolis as it was fifty-three years ago, when it was served by ten different railroads and one major airline. No wonder things were so great back then.

I sat outside the room all afternoon and into evening. It is a busy hospital, with constant traffic in the halls. That did not seem to bother Betty. In all that time, not one person, doctor, nurse, or volunteer passed me without a smile or a greeting. The atmosphere seemed to encourage patients to feel better. I have seen hospitals where the staff is grouchy. There are explanations for this, I think, but no excuses.

I was a nineteen-year-old corpsman at Oak Knoll, the naval hospital in Oakland, California, when I first saw a man die. I don't recall the cause of his death. I later saw men die from wounds suffered in the Pacific war. I saw men die from complications of malaria and from complications of diabetes. I saw men die from meningitis, spinal or cerebral. I saw a man die from leukemia.

But most of the wounded and diseased young men walked out of the hospital healthy, probably something like 99 percent of them did. Many of them undoubtedly are grandfathers now, living the first years of retirement.

Since that time, I have thought of hospitals as places of cure and relief, not as funeral parlors. Patients have enough to contend with, their fears and their pain, without being treated by soreheads. The hospital Betty was in was a place of cure and relief.

Mike and I called Betty's mother at the nursing home and Laura and Andy in New York. We went out for dinner. When we returned to the hospital, Betty was awake and smiling. The patch was off her unwounded eye. She had finished her supper.

"The Simpsons" snarled on her roommate's television set. Betty said her roommate was a young woman recovering from an extremely painful operation. The young woman probably hurt too much to read. She certainly was entitled to "The Simpsons," "Oprah," the jolly game shows, all of it.

The doctor will see Betty tomorrow. She undoubtedly will be able to leave the hospital. Betty says the nurses who care for her have voices like angels.

❖ ❖ ❖ ❖ ❖

Friday July 26

Betty phoned a little after eight this morning. She is ready to play football. The doctor told her she could leave at any time. What she wants is to be back on the island.

I have felt the same sense of joy and relief only once before in my life. In 1972, around Christmas, Betty discovered a lump in her breast. She went to the hospital for surgery around the New Year. Russ had just died, and Helen spent the holidays with us. She stayed over to help me with the children. I remember the night before the surgery, Betty in the hospital, Helen and I listening to the clock tick in the living room. She knit, and I pretended to read. I showed her a "Dennis the Menace" panel from that day's newspaper. Dennis is sitting in a chair in the corner, facing the wall, and he says, "I don't like the way this year is gettin' off to a start."

The next day we learned the lump was benign. Now I experienced the kind of happiness and gratitude I felt back then. Mike and I hurried to the hospital. We waited with Betty for a painkiller. Betty insisted she is not in much pain.

We made only one stop, for lunch, on our race through sunshine back to the island. We ate hamburgers, and I placed a medicinal drop in Betty's eye and changed her patch. She has a pretty good shiner and her eye is a little bloody.

❖ ❖ ❖ ❖ ❖

Saturday, July 27

Betty tried reading her Italian novel. She cannot see clearly, and it hurts her to move her eye.

She is listening to *Hot Money* by Dick Francis on her tape player. It is one of several books on tape a neighbor loaned her. She has never read Dick Francis before, and she is enjoying the book.

❖ ❖ ❖ ❖ ❖

Wednesday, July 31

Betty announced today, "I can read!"
She is a bad patient. We have to natter at her to keep her

eye patched when she is outdoors, as the doctor insisted she do. She offers feeble excuses she would not accept from the children. She claims sitting in the yard is like sitting in our cabin, although the dust blows in the yard and insects zoom about.

Betty now applies her own drops and changes the patch, dismissing the retired corpsman. When she washes her hair in the lake, I help her rinse, keeping her hair away from her eyes. "Isn't that sweet," a friend purred. "She waits on you all the time. Now you can help her."

Friday, August 2

The ophthalmologist says Betty is ready to start sparring with heavy gloves.

Good-byes

Saturday, August 3

Amy and Mike left for New York shortly after eleven o'clock this morning, in a steady rain.

The rain began about 3:00 A.M., and it fell as remorselessly as a waterfall through the night and into the day. I woke up about four and listened to the rain on the roof, Betty breathing beside me. I was thankful nothing called me from the island this day. I am retired.

Rain often accompanies island leave-taking. It seems to me that most autumns, as Betty and I close the cabin, we squint into a drenching rain as we look up to hang the shutters. I take this as a sign the island gods are angry that we leave. When it is sunny, I take it as a sign the island gods are angry and taunt us with a reminder of the beauty we are leaving.

Amy and Mike arrived fifteen days ago, she on vacation. He has quit his job in Superior and is going to Los Angeles to look for newspaper work. He returned to New York, then he and his sister drove twenty-seven sleepless hours from the city in Mike's spiffy red GEO, which is about the size of a bathtub, with Amy's two large black dogs in the back seat, the saintly Emma squeezed into a corner, the delinquent Buck stretched out, selfish and carsick.

No one makes me laugh, or think, harder than my children. We have had a lot of fun the last two weeks, in spite of Betty's torn retina. It is always painful to say good-bye to the children. Life consists of little farewells. Husband and wife part each day; children leave for school each day. Farewells are so routine we accept these partings as if we had forever with each other.

I've been leaving this island almost every year since 1930, and it always hurts. I remember feeling the fist in the throat as a small boy after the boat picked us up to carry us to the mainland, one sister looking back at the island because she could not bear not to, the other sister facing forward because she could not bear to see the island recede. Wherever I looked, my eyes were full of tears.

Scenes from a home movie: Betty and I leave the island together for the first time. I am running the motor, she is pregnant. A year later, it is the same situation except that now she is holding the baby Amy as Mother waves good-bye from the dock. It is the last time I saw my mother on the island. She died the following winter. Then, Betty and I leave with two, three, finally four small children under a pale morning moon. It is cold and the children burrow into us for warmth and solace in the open boat.

How many farewells?

I saw in a newspaper that we are just four days away from midsummer. The state will close beaches later in the month, but Betty and I will not be leaving until the end of

September. I can almost recapture the childhood illusion that time stands still here in the green world, for Betty and I sleep under charms that transcend the years:

Over our heads is Mother's *Anachronistic Topography of Vassar Female College—1861–1928.* On the wall to our left are two watercolors my grandmother left me, *Mr. Pecksniff Leaves for London* under blue English skies and *Mr. Pecksniff and the Miss Pecksniffs Return from London* in a gray rain. I studied these paintings years before I knew what a Pecksniff is, which is all around us. But these charms are false; they cannot delay our departure by so much as a tick of the clock.

After Amy and Mike left, Betty and I read, ate lunch, goofed around, an All-America vacation day. We walked to the next bay and visited Betty's sister and her family, who arrived on the island yesterday. The rain ceased. We chatted on the path with friends who left the island briefly and are, briefly, back, and with a friend who is leaving after two weeks but will be back for weekends and, in fact, will be back to say good-bye when Betty and I leave.

The island now is busier with comings and goings than at any time this summer. I am retired, on a kind of perpetual vacation, but summer remains a season punctuated by farewells.

Harry
Wednesday, August 7

Damn. Damn. Damn. Damn. Damn.

Harry Reasoner died last night.

We learned about it this morning, which was soon enough. Betty and I made our weekly trip to the mainland to visit the grocery, the laundry, and the hardware store. We picked up our mail and a neighbor's Minneapolis newspaper at the Bush administration mail drop. There was the front-page headline VETERAN JOURNALIST HARRY REASONER DIES, accompanied by a color photo.

The story said Harry contracted pneumonia after brain surgery to remove a blood clot. He had been in the hospital six weeks. He was sixty-eight. The news was heartbreaking and a shock, even though it was not unexpected. Harry was in the hospital when Betty and I left New York, seriously ill enough that a friend promised to let me know if Harry's condition worsened.

But I didn't think Harry would die. I mean, I knew he was mortal, but standing near the lake under the brilliant sky, I thought, Damn it, I just can't believe that Harry is dead. I cannot believe I will not see that warm and derisive smile again.

In fiction, at a time of death, the protagonist thinks "irrelevantly." What other way is there to think about the death of someone you love? What is relevant that you can think? He is better off out of this mean world? He has gone to a better place? He ran a good race?

Betty heard me read the headline out loud and ran over to me and held me. Then I walked to the boat landing office and called Andy Rooney in New York. He and Harry were close. I learned more about writing for television from the two of them than from anyone else I ever worked with.

(The biggest thing Harry taught me was not to underestimate an audience's intelligence or to overestimate the attention an audience may be giving your words. An old newsman once told me he knew an editorial writer who worked with a photo of a moron on his desk, as a reminder of the kind of people he was trying to reach. I thought that was a horrid story, and I still do. Harry never assumed he knew more than the people he was writing for. The show we worked on was on the air in the morning, though, and Harry figured that our audience was likely to be distracted by children, doorbells, telephone calls, and other blessings.)

Now there was not much Andy could say. Harry had fallen at home and apparently never came out of the coma after an operation to remove a clot which had formed on his brain. Andy gave me some Reasoner family telephone numbers.

I had to get the news somewhere, and it probably was right to get it outside a village in the midwest. Harry was from small-town Iowa, and he never lost the small-town twang or many of the small-town values, good and bad.

He and I had worked up a number of small-town routines, into which we would fall even if we hadn't seen each other for months. They would look painful on paper. They were based, loosely, on the observations of the Iowa writer Richard Bissell, author of 7½ Cents, which became the Broadway musical *The Pajama Game,* and more important for Harry and me, author of *A Stretch on the River,* which is one of the best books I have ever read about American life.

Harry and I could as easily have based a routine on overheard talk in New York elevators or on New York streets, but we shared this midwestern bond and an admiration for the works of Bissell.

All this morning, as Betty and I ran our errands in the small town, I thought about Harry. I stood paralyzed before shelves of soup, thinking, irrelevantly, about Harry.

I recalled a day in the '70s when the army worms had defoliated the island and the late summer sun turned the trees orange. A forester appeared before me and asked, "Are you the one who works for CBS?" I said, "Yes," thinking, Here it comes, we are all Commies or part of an infernal cult or subverting the morals of children. But what he said was, "I've got a bone to pick with you. Why did you take 'Gunsmoke' off the air?" I said I didn't have any voice in that decision, and besides "Gunsmoke" had been on the air since the turn of the century.

I told that story to Harry. CBS produced a lot of junk on the people's air back then but the network was defined by "Gunsmoke" and "I Love Lucy" and Walter Cronkite. And Harry. (And Dan Rather covered the Nixon White House, and Morley Safer covered Vietnam.)

The first time I saw Harry I figured he was something special. Betty and I had been married a couple of years before we acquired our first television set. We quickly became fans of a CBS broadcast called "Camera Three," which appeared on Sunday mornings. There was a five-minute news broadcast which came on the air just before "Camera Three."

One Sunday this white-haired fellow appeared on the news show. He had a face full of character and a back-home voice. He said nothing of much importance had happened in the great world overnight, so he wanted to talk about a man who had just died in Minneapolis. He said if you weren't from Minnesota, the name Cedric Adams wouldn't mean anything to you. He then explained why the death of this newspaper columnist and radio talker was significant.

I hadn't heard anything like that before. I thought, Here comes this fellow on a national news program and says nothing routinely big happened, so let me tell you about something else that is big in its own way. I learned his name when he signed off.

Around that time I read a *Times* story about Harry Reasoner, a television figure who was attracting notice with his wry, midwestern sense of humor. (This is the sort of praise that makes some midwesterners smile, wryly.) He and John Merriman, the news editor for Walter Cronkite, had concocted an All-Cliché football team. It starred Mounting Tension, the Sherpa running back, and Bodes Ill, the Norwegian tackle, and Grinding Poverty, the Eurasian split end, and God knows who else, Fragile Peace, the lovely cheerleader.

My first job in television was writing a program called "Eye on New York" for WCBS-TV, the CBS station. In the summer, we had a succession of different hosts for the show. One day I was writing a script while the producer and others were out on location, a trailer park, I think.

In those days, scripts were copied in big letters on what were called cue cards, which were held just out of camera range, making the correspondent articulate if not fluent. Late in the day, the producer rushed into my office, bug-eyed. "You should have seen this fellow, John," he said. "He looked at your script for a couple of minutes, then said every line into the camera perfectly. No cue cards. Every comma."

The correspondent was Harry, of course. (He may still have been classified as a reporter. He once told me the day he was promoted to CBS News correspondent was the proudest of his life. That pride about CBS is how we felt in "Gun-smoke" days.)

Not long after that, we were recording an "Eye" in the studio when Harry read a line of mine that made him laugh out loud. I don't remember the line, but I remember that explosive laugh, which was better than a raise.

We were having drinks one afternoon, after a taping. Harry said he was about to leave WCBS-TV to do a daily show called "Calendar" for the network. He said the head writer for the new show would be a man named Andy Rooney and asked me if I had ever heard of him. I hadn't, but I hadn't heard of any television writers, I suppose, except Paddy Chayefsky and Rod Serling. Harry said Andy had written for Arthur Godfrey and was a talented man. It seems improbable, even as I think back on it, that there was a time when an adult American had never heard of Andy Rooney.

Harry brought me over to work on "Calendar" after one of the three writers left. "Calendar" lasted for two years. Other good people worked there, but its style was shaped by Harry and Andy. It was the most literate place I worked for in television. (Harry and John had another list called "Faint Praise.")

Harry and Andy were tough to work with. They were never unpleasant but they were demanding. "Dumb it down," Andy told me once after I had produced a truly literary effort. The idea was that the viewer has to get what you write in the first place—he cannot go back and check the words. There is nothing condescending in this. I am a lover of print, and I see writing every day that simply would not have done for "Calendar."

Harry and Andy murdered clichés. They admired grace and laughter. It was exciting to work there. When I learned how well Harry wrote, with elegance and simplicity, I was embarrassed at the idea of putting words in his mouth. He was secure enough to be easy with praise.

Harry and I didn't agree about everything. He admired James Gould Cozzens more than I did. But in a contest on "Calendar" to name the worst novel written by a major living author, Harry chose *By Love Possessed.* I held out for *Across the River and into the Trees,* which finished second in weighted voting.

Harry hated Edmund Wilson, whom I liked. "Wilson can't write, Mosedale," he told me. Harry couldn't be convinced that college football hadn't suffered a mortal blow when Bernie Bierman was retired as head coach at the University of Minnesota in 1949.

But we shared a provincial, almost secretive understanding of Fitzgerald, a love for midwestern lawns blue at dusk, and slim girls outlined against orange windows, a girl in a slip drifting through a smokey room above the laundromat on Main Street (very unFitz, that), and sleigh rides under a winter moon. (Harry had written a novel called *Tell Me About Women.*)

During the run of "Calendar," an executive at WCBS-TV, knowing I loved football, asked me to write a special for the New York Giants–Green Bay Packers championship games. In those pallid days, we didn't have Super Bowls, only championship games.

Harry was the star of the show. We had fun with it, a kind of fun it would be hard to duplicate today. We seemed more relaxed back then. Pro football had just become the hot ticket in town. Harry told me for years that he heard more comment about *Pro Football Madness: What's Going on Here?* than about anything else he had done. (Television producers would die without ":") *Variety* praised the show extravagantly, which led to me getting a job, just when I needed it, with CBS Sports, when "Calendar" went off the air.

I didn't see much of Harry in recent years. We worked in different shops. He even left CBS for a time. He didn't live in the city, except for a brief period. We were busy, in the damnable way you get too busy to see people you love.

Even when we didn't see each other, though, we stayed in touch. For one thing, we mailed each other so many examples of the misuse of the word *hopefully* that it is to be hoped I will never use the word again, even correctly. I think I found Harry's favorite when I sent him a story quoting a grief-stricken man as saying, "Hopefully we'll send the body home Monday."

We sometimes met for lunch. Harry ate lunch with another friend. The two of them started lunch with a couple of martinis, as did I before I quit drinking. After I quit drinking and, even more, after I quit smoking, the wait for lunch through those martinis was just too long, no matter how entertaining the talk.

People gossiped for years about Harry's drinking. I know he drank because I drank with him. Often we would stop for a drink after "Calendar" went off the air for the day, the waiters setting up tables for lunch, the bartender readying his tools. "There is nothing more immoral about a drink at ten o'clock in the morning than there is in a drink at ten o'clock at night," said Harry. I drank to that.

I quit drinking. Harry didn't. I had no choice.

When I found myself briefly jobless in 1972, Harry offered me work on a new program at ABC. I was immediately offered more money and more security for a job at CBS, and I accepted that job. Except for a ritual curse when I took him to lunch, Harry was fine.

The last time I saw Harry was at my retirement dinner. It must have been an effort for him to come in from Connecticut. He did not look well, but he was there, and he made a gracious speech.

Gracious, now that I think of it, was the right word for the Harry I knew. I read in one of the obituaries today that Harry once paid a two-hundred-dollar hospital bill for a friend at a time when Harry was a twenty-seven-dollar-a-week reporter. I wouldn't believe that story about a lot of people, but I believe it about Harry.

That's the least of it. Harry was a colleague and a mentor and a friend. He was one of Mike's godfathers. He was an inspiration.

He got the lead today in the *Star Tribune* and, I am told, in one of the New York newspapers. That would please the old Minneapolis newspaperman. He would smile (wryly) but he would be pleased.

I don't remember ever feeling sadder.

I am writing this on the island in late afternoon. It threatened rain earlier, but now the sky is pink and orange, and there may be a sunset. I can't believe I won't see Harry smile again.

Baby

Tuesday, August 13

The old gent, retired, plays with his grandchild. How many rosy versions of that have we seen in paintings, photographs, movies, commercials, advertisements? Isn't that how the God-father died?

Laura arrived with Molly last evening. They flew in from New York. Molly was two months old to the day. She is so much a part of our life she already seems eternal.

Betty and I drove to pick them up under Molly-blue skies. We stopped for groceries on the way. It is terrible to be sixty-five years old, money in your pocket, standing before bags full of Three Musketeers bars, recalling childhood dreams, and then letting your wretched willpower get the best of you.

At the mall, Betty bought wine glasses, and I bought a late-summer-sale bathing suit. I picked up a couple of pop tapes, and we consumed butterscotch milkshakes that were, simply, perfect. Anything that tastes so good obviously is good for you.

The airport terminal is being rebuilt, and we waited in a makeshift area. I might have found that depressing but not when I was waiting for our daughter and her daughter.

The plane arrived, disgorging the world's fourth largest army. Laura finally stepped out with Molly in her arms, in radiance. All babies supposedly look alike, but not as grandparents see them. Molly looks only like Molly. Her eyes are a deeper blue than when I last saw her. She smiles. Cynics might dispute that, but cynics know only half the story.

The sun set in a giant red ball beyond the pines as we returned to the island. It seemed an auspicious first crossing for Molly. Back in the cabin, we ate and visited, gaping at Molly as darkness fell and gaped more at Molly while Laura opened gifts for the baby left by islanders.

In the jaded world of television, the president of the United States is briefly noted as he visits a broadcast studio. What attracts attention in a television studio is a heavyweight champion of the world or certain singers, Miss Peggy Lee, for instance.

Molly, two months, commands that kind of notice in our cabin. I am sure little monarchs reign under other roofs on this island, at this moment.

I suppose sensitive souls in each generation feel guilty about the world they leave their children and grandchildren. I looked at little Molly in her recliner last night as I read stories about increased violence in our land and estimates that if medical costs continue to increase at their present rate, they will account for the entire Gross National Product by the year 2040.

I took Molly's small hand. "Kid," I said, "it's up to you. By the year 2040, you will be forty-nine years old. Maybe you will have figured out how to hold down medical costs, or how to convince Americans to stop plugging each other."

Betty and Laura and Molly are picnicking today with other islanders at a place where we have picnicked for generations. We do not leave her much of a world, but we leave her a pretty good island.

Party Time

Yesterday was the midway point of the amount of time Betty and I have to spend on the island this year.

Betty was not happy to be reminded of this. The second half of anything—a play, a football game—almost always goes faster than the first half. The days crowded with doing nothing will speed to a close.

This seems ungrateful, I know, when retirement is giving us a full summer on the island. But I think of a friend who said at halftime of the first pro football game of the year, "My God, the season is slipping away from us." Fifteen weeks and some forty games lay ahead, but he was right.

Betty and I spent much of the day on the mainland. Betty saw her eye doctor. Her distance vision, with glasses, is 20/20. She sees a lot of garbage with her left eye, and it still gives her some pain. The doctor said this is to be expected. He fitted her with fancy new bifocals.

We bought groceries and wine. We did not enter a book store, but I acquired four new books. This is how things get out of control.

Back on the island, we just had time to swim before a Shakespearean storm crashed around our heads. A small cabin in a great storm is wonderfully comforting. Betty and Laura and I watched the storm with admiration. Molly had no opinion.

Laura said that while Betty and I were in town an island friend brought some guests to see our cabin. He paused dramatically in our living room and announced, "This cabin is frozen in time! This is how my grandfather lived!" He led his visitors to the pump room. Laura allowed them to pump water. He pointed to the outhouse. We may put in for landmark status.

The rain eased, the lake calmed, and the four of us set off for a cocktail party on another shore. There were about thirty people there. Molly was admired. She accepted it like a lady. One of the afternoon visitors to our cabin said to me, "I was asking your wife if you ever thought of bringing that outhouse into the house." I told him we had a family Un-American Activities Committee and we would traduce anyone suggesting indoor plumbing in our cabin.

Parties on the island are informal because it is an informal place. I would not think of "dropping in" on someone in New York. I call first. On the island we drop in and are dropped in on all the time.

We attended a Texas Night party last week, originated by two of my nieces, who have Texas roots. We were to come dressed as Texans. I wore a straw hat and jeans. It was too hot for duck boots, which would have been a lame imitation in any case. I wore my press credentials from the 1984 Republican convention in Dallas. I also carried what I called "a

Texas Bible," *God's Coach,* the biography of Tom Landry. The husband of one niece, a Texan, strung himself out in Christmas tree lights and came as the Electric Horseman. Betty's nephew played the guitar for a community sing.

Friends urged us to stage a New York Night party next summer. We will.

Everything up here reminds me of something else. Corny, homegrown entertainment is an island tradition. Back in the early thirties, shadow plays were popular. The host strung a sheet over a wire. The audience sat in the dark. Backlit by kerosene lamps, shadows stretched grotesquely on the sheet. A popular skit was "The Operation," in which a shadow surgeon removed from a shadow patient, who was stretched upon a table, rakes, spades, spoons, axes, hoes, and, finally, a wheelbarrow.

A couple of summers ago, Betty and I threw a dance party at her mother's cabin, where it is possible to clear a little space. We danced to tapes of Goodman and Shaw and Miller and to Viennese waltzes. The disadvantage of this is that there are not many ballroom dancers up here. The advantage is that you are sixteen again.

Where the Time Goes

Sunday, August 25

"Where does the time go?"

The rhetorical question about island summers may be un-answerable. Am I less busy doing nothing as we always do on the island than I am, retired, doing nothing in New York? People who complain about the emptiness of retirement never seem to complain in a vacation setting. They are not bothered doing nothing except where they were in the habit of doing something.

Life is not bookkeeping, but to keep track of life, I de-cided to account for my daily activities during one week of retirement. We ate, read, swam, and walked each day. I tried to mention only events that separate one summer's day from another.

Monday, August 19

I turned on the radio as I fixed myself breakfast and heard that Gorbachev is out in a coup. Even earthshaking news from the outside world seems remote from the cabin. That is a condition of islandness, a blessing and a curse. In the city there always is a sense of involvement, although the events occur far away. Reading about or hearing or watching news in the city makes me a participant, or, at least, an involved spectator. I so far have not missed the newsroom for a tick of a clock. I wonder what my former colleagues are up to with this story, but I am glad I am not there to find out. On the island, I delude myself that I am an island.

It is easier to remember birthdays and anniversaries than it is to remember historic dates. I was a sailor in San Francisco when the biggest war in history ended, celebrating with a girl. I swore I would never forget the date. But it slipped by me last week.

Now the Communist world seems to be disappearing like picnic ants in a rain. Communism was our great national nightmare for more than forty years, and it was only a boogeyman. On the island, as these tremendous events transpire in the Soviet Union, the big news remains children, dogs, visitors, and the weather.

Betty and I talked some about Gorbachev and listened to *Il Trovatore* as we did dishes this morning. We always wash and dry the previous day's dishes after breakfast. *Washing dishes with my sweetie at the kitchen sink.* Try warbling that over the automatic. How many people remember Frank Crumit?

Living alone on the island in the winter of 1953–54, I listened to an hour and a quarter of fifteen-minute network radio news each evening as I cooked and ate my dinner. The bias of the broadcasts ranged from the mild liberalism of John

W. Vandercook, who was sponsored by the AFL-CIO, to the reactionary meditations of Fulton Lewis, Jr. Working more toward the middle ground were Gabriel Heatter and Lowell Thomas. This made for great listening, of a sort that is no longer available. I indulged in arguments, alone in the cabin, bellowing at the radio.

I listened at the end of each evening to Edward R. Murrow, who I believed reported the news with fairness and put the day in perspective. I was a CBS man before I so much as thought of working for CBS.

Much of the news that fall and winter speculated on the successor to Stalin, who had recently died. I heard a good deal about Malenkov, Bulganin, Kaganovich, and Beria. The voices of authority dismissed the clown Khrushchev, who was only a kind of window dummy. Now someone somewhere certainly said that Khrushchev would bury his rivals, but I didn't hear it.

All this confirmed my youthful suspicion of foreign correspondence, where there always are more experts than there are reporters. I am recalling the experience of that winter as I try to make sense of what is happening with Gorbachev. I think the first expert I heard today is the one to stick with. He said he was stunned by the coup, didn't expect it, and didn't know what to make of it.

Betty and I walked to the next bay to visit with Matt, who arrived yesterday. He, Laura, and Molly are staying in the cabin Betty grew up in. There is a telephone in this cabin. I was waiting for a call from a high school friend, who is traveling across the country with his wife. I get word they will arrive tomorrow.

Mike called from New York. He cannot find a couple of Shakespeare tapes I told him were missing from a group I brought up here. I miscalculated. The tapes are here. I do not understand how I did anything so stupid. Am I getting foolish with age? I tell myself I might have made the same kind of mistake when I was twenty, which is true.

I read in the *Verdi Companion,* but mostly I watch Molly and watch my wife and our daughter watch Molly, who is the little sun around which the solar system of this family revolves.

Betty, Laura, Matt, and Molly all have errands on the mainland. After they leave, I walk back to our cabin, listening to Leontyne Price sing Verdi. I translate from the Italian in my Mike Tyson biography. It is slow going. I think of the aged I. F. Stone, who sometimes spent a day translating a single sentence from the ancient Greek, except that he translated a shaping philosophy and I translate fight journalism in a modern language. Betty zips through Italian novels as I slog along.

I think I have little talent for learning language. I also think of how much more Italian I know now than I knew a year ago. It is important to compare myself with myself.

Not much on the radio about the Soviet Union. The story has not advanced from this morning. The water is warmer than the air as I swim.

Betty returned, bearing food, newspapers, and other necessities of life. I read the *St. Paul Pioneer-Press* while she swam. Nothing as yet on the Soviet shake-up. The Mets have completed their first all-losing road trip ever. I find that hard to credit. They have lost ten straight. Didn't they do worse than that in their dreary opening years?

I read a column saying that the Democrats are doomed if they choose a liberal as their presidential candidate next year. I read a column saying the Democrats are doomed if they do not choose a liberal as their presidential candidate next year.

Laura, Matt, and Molly came to our cabin for dinner. We drove them back to their cabin in the boat, under a balloon of a moon on the moving waters. Betty and I walked home by moonlight. The warm wind takes our breath away. She is like a girlfriend. It's only been thirty-five years.

Tuesday, August 20

I awoke in a night that seemed black beyond the possibility of light. The wind was high in the pines. Splashing waves bring the eternal note of sadness in. It is an auditory experience except for the pine air.

143

Betty and I don't really get the day underway before 10:00 A.M. We hear radio reports on whatever it is that is happening in the Soviet Union. Troops march on parliament, troops prepare to defend it. Yeltsin is on the telephone to Western leaders. I recall the Hungarian revolt in 1956, leaders of that revolution pleading for help from the West as the tanks rolled in.

Betty and I mount a major walk, up and down hill, around swamps. It is still in the woods, and hot. There are few insects left. An occasional, pathetic mosquito tries to attack. We come out on the opposite side of the island, visit friends with lively views on what is happening in the Soviet Union.

We pushed on to visit what is called "the big tree" because that is what it is. We figure this white pine measures about fourteen feet around the trunk. Seen from a distance, it towers above all other trees in the forest. Children climb the tree to its top and report they can see all the island from up there. I seem to remember when the tree was called The Sentinel, but is there a forest in the land where the tallest tree is not called The Sentinel, inspirer of bad verse?

Betty and I talked to Mike on the phone that evening. He told us a committee is now running things in the Soviet Union. He said it sounds like the Committee for Public Safety in the French revolution, functionaries whose function is killing people.

Wednesday, August 21

The horizon was pink with dawn as Betty and I swam. We could not locate news on the radio. We walked down to Molly's place, as I think of it, to await a phone call from my high school friend. I take along *A Winter's Tale*, for no particular reason. "Reade him, therefore; and againe, and againe," urged Heminge and Condell, and I try my best.

The day, which dawned so clear, suddenly is overcast. I hope it doesn't rain, for I mean to walk my friends around a little, not to the big tree which would be a snipe hunt, but enough to give them a sense of the place.

I was reading Time's announcement in *A Winter's Tale* that sixteen years have passed even as he speaks. The phone rang, and my high school friend said, "We are here, wherever 'here' is."

Betty and I crossed the lake to pick up my friend and his wife. The sky was clear. The clouds have passed. I had not seen my friends for five years, not since I was in California with the evening news, but then we have seen each other only a few times over the decades. They told us the Soviet coup seemed to be unraveling, according to their car radio. The episode, history in the making, was hard to follow in the green and blue world.

We returned to the island, fed our guests lunch, and led them through the woods and out to a sandy shore. My friend reminded me that it would be fifty years next February that we met in Miss Marcella Zeman's sophomore English class at Riverside High School in Milwaukee, he having just moved to Milwaukee from St. Louis.

The trunk of my friend's 1935 blue Nash held up to three cases of Schlitz. In the mysterious manner of youth, we called his car "The Green Dragon." He and I were in a one-act play that won a state forensics award when we acted it in the university theater at Madison. I played a bachelor rover with tales of glamour and adventure. He played a homebody, dazzled by my stories. A pretty classmate acted his wife, smiling a Mona Lisa smile at curtain as he vowed to join me in my pointless odyssey.

After all these years, he recalled an impossible line he had to say, "We shall get drenched, gloriously drenched." I remember only that I leaned rakishly on the piano, a prop pipe in my mouth, thinking perhaps of Leslie Howard.

❖ ❖ ❖ ❖ ❖

My friend's wife spoke about how clear the lake looked and how unlittered our island trails were. I wondered that anyone who lived in Idaho, which I always think of as unspoiled, never having been there, would be surprised by un-littered ways. I read not long ago that there no longer is any pure water in this country; only water that is less polluted than other water.

We returned as a worker finished up a new gray-water system for the cabin. It has been a quarter of a century since the last time we had this done. I will not be involved the next time. The thought somehow amuses me. Perhaps because we are seeing my high school friend, I remember something I read my freshman or sophomore year. I don't have the exact words anymore, but Joyce Kilmer wrote something like, "The earth to me seemed self-sufficient, and my brief sojourn there one trembling opportunity for joy." I didn't know a mantra from a V-eight engine, but if I had, that would have been my mantra. It was all the explanation for life I needed. Now I was warmed by the recollection of that thought and the strength it gave me in my youth.

Laura and Matt went to the mainland for dinner. Betty and I sat with Molly for the first time. In that circumstance, it helps if any other adults present are parents, too, and my friends have five children, so nothing Molly might have done would have surprised them. But she was uncomplaining and the adults had a good talk.

Thursday, August 11

My friend was at the pump room table, reading my book about the 1927 New York Yankees when I arose this morning. We got to talking about the minor-league Milwaukee Brewers of our high school years. We used to cut class to see them play on opening day. That and drinking beer was about as delinquent as we got.

Betty and I took our friends over to the mainland for their departure. In the mail I found a gift from a friend who lives in these parts. He is an amateur trader in unconsidered trifles, and he has sent me a battered, rusting tin truck, its wheels missing. Columbia Broadcasting System it says on the sides. We were delighted with the gift. Betty said she will build a shelf for it.

We were back in the cabin in time for lunch. Gorbachev appeared to be returned to power. We listened to his news conference as we did dishes. An analyst said Gorbachev began the conference shaken, groping for answers. Why not? People he thought were friends betrayed him.

Betty and I swam in a lake that only now, in late August, seemed to be cold. The sun still rode high in the late afternoon sky.

Harry used to tell about a man who lived on an island in the South Pacific. Life was effortless. Each day the sun rose in splendor. One morning the man emerged from his hut, looked at the rising sun, and said, "Another perfect goddamned day" and shot himself. The weather gods make sure you will not tire of ceaseless sunshine in the north woods.

Our dinner company tonight included Miss Molly, her parents, and a couple I think of as major islanders, a private classification. They frequently spend winter weekends here, when the temperature can drop to fifty below zero, in a cabin only slightly more advanced than ours. (They have a telephone.) Another major islander we visited with recently is a woman who explained she must spend at least three months a year on the island, without so much as a single trip to the mainland. (Her husband likes to run the boat and shop.)

When the children were little, I established in my mother's name a trophy to be awarded the child who made the fewest trips to town. I needn't have worried. None of our children was ambitious for mainland visits. All my trophy did was make it more difficult for Betty to find hands to help her shop once I was back in New York. If I had established a Dumb Idea trophy, I would have retired it myself.

After dinner, I called Mike in New York. He told me about the Crown Heights riots in Brooklyn, Jews and blacks at each other. I had heard nothing of this. The riots, although they occur in my hometown, seem as remote as events in the Soviet Union, as remote as the ninety-five-degree heat Mike says buries New York.

The morning sky was gray. This would have been a fine day for rain. We expect no company, and rain might encourage me to stay indoors and think and write, but the sun soon was shining.

Molly dropped in, accompanied by her parents. Matt gave me a test from the St. Paul newspaper. The test demonstrated that, since I looked to my left while pondering a question, I belonged to a group which tends to show "greater fluency in writing, study the humanities, imagine more vividly . . . are more sociable, musical and religious and more likely to become alcoholics."

Molly led her parents to a walk in the woods. Betty painted the front stoop. She will not let me paint on account of my asthma, which I acquired late in life and which gets slightly worse each year. (I am never sure of this usage. It seems to me the asthma gets better. I get worse.)

I listened to *Hamlet.* The critic John Mason Brown, more than forty years ago, wrote, "I can never remember, even when I have come to the theatre fresh from a rereading of the script, the precise sequence of the scenes or the exact moment when this soliloquy, or great speech, or memorable line, will burst upon the ear." I reflected on this comforting confession, a retired fellow too much in the sun, sitting on a swing and looking over a tree-covered bank to the lake.

We heard on the radio that Yeltsin will no longer allow Communist publications, such as *Pravda,* to be published in Russia. It seems to me the earth should crack at such news, but Communism's last rites get no more air time than the Minnesota State Fair, where it rained today.

After dinner, Betty and I used Helen's boat to tow our canoe to a small lake nearby. We make a short portage.

We canoe around the lake as the moon edges up in the sky. The hour is just after sunset. The moon is pale, obscured by a pile of clouds that glow pink and gray in the reflected sunset. We canoe in silence, except for the sound of a fishing boat that trolls across the lake.

The woods are black in the dusk. The moon now rises silver over the line of pines around the lake. The fishermen depart, rolling their boat on logs through the portage to the big lake.

There are no sounds except insect hum and the plash of canoe paddles. We are close to a blue heron. He is fishing, not ten yards from us. He flies off a short distance, then settles back to fishing. He freezes as we glide by.

The loons have fallen silent the past couple of days. We no longer hear birdsong at morning and in the evening, as we did just a yesterday ago. The moon is high and golden when we portage out of the lake and pick up Helen's boat where it is moored and tow the canoe home.

Saturday, August 24

Mysterious laws govern household affairs. It seems to take roughly the same time to wash and dry dishes for two people or for a party. I read somewhere that the cook in today's efficiency kitchen takes more steps than did yesterday's cook with a wood stove and hand pump. This seems unlikely. But I notice that folks with all the advantages don't appear to have any more time to loaf than do we who linger in the dark ages.

I am determined to take time to read. In *Benny Goodman,* I learn that the *Chicago Tribune* reported in 1935 that Goodman would "introduce his swing band at the Urban room." This is the earliest use of *swing* Goodman's biographer can find as applied to music. Goodman was reluctant to integrate black musicians into the band. He was not prejudiced as to race, but he was aware that prejudices existed. The prospect was more daunting than the reality. Blacks appeared with the band, music improved, and there was no major disturbance.

The radio informed us that the Soviet Union continues to unravel. The West looks on without firing a shot. This is the way Communism ends, with a whimper.

Betty prepared dinner for ten or maybe twelve guests, if

Mike and his pal Richard arrive from New York on time. I worked on this journal, which I am pleased to be keeping since it reminds me of simple pleasures. I would remember high points such as Molly's birth and my retirement dinner and low points such as Betty's eye surgery and Harry's death. But only a journal catches the diurnal beat of life.

Betty interrupted her preparations to invite a couple in for a cool drink on this hot day. They are circumnavigating the island. I marvel at how Betty can take time out and appear so relaxed with all the things she must get done. She is like the classic boxer who, as they say, fights within himself, that is, knows his limits and maintains control.

Betty and I swam before our dinner guests arrived, a party of six. Laura, Matt, and Molly joined us. After cocktails, we jammed along the long table in The Pump Room. I thought of the blazing summers of the depression when this table always seemed lined with friends of my mother's and sisters' and all the excited talk and laughter and cut-glass jeroboams of iced tea.

Now there were four male lawyers at the table, and five women also with interesting jobs (and one retired newsman), so it was not an evening punctuated by long silences. We continued visiting in the living room after dinner. Michael and Richard showed up looking tired and happy. Mike said all his worldly possessions were in our little boat. The evening became an uproar.

Our guests departed, to beat an expected rain. We talked with the boys, and the storm broke. It was a satisfying display of thunder, lightning, and all the rain there is to go to bed by. Betty and I agree there is no place in the world this good for us.

❖ ❖ ❖ ❖ ❖

Sunday, August 25

We awoke in sadness to a beautiful day. It is a day of departure. After dishes, I take to the swing in the yard and sip coffee in a soft, strong wind, listening to Sinatra. The boys emerge, wander into the yard, and we talk. A girl awaits Mike in Los Angeles, and I hope a newsman's job does, too. Betty, Mike, and I head for the next bay and our melancholy errand.

Laura and Matt are all packed. Molly is full of smiles. We are all aboard Helen's boat when the motor proves to be as dead as Marley. There is brief, communal panic, balanced by Laura's conviction that there are worse fates than missing a plane and being forced to spend an extra day on the island.

A friend arrives in his big boat on an errand at the next dock. He gets us across the lake in style. We arrive at the airport in plenty of time, damn it. Laura, Matt, and Molly fly off into the sun. It will be four weeks before we see them. I am sure that by then Molly will be playing Bach fugues and scorning her old grandfather.

Betty and I drowned our sorrows in butterscotch shakes. The wind has died and it is ninety in our living room when we get back to the island. The boys disappear with friends. Betty and I disappear for a nap. This is a principal difference between youth and age.

Later the boys and I discuss news from the five Sunday papers I bought at the mall. We talk more about football than we do about the Soviet Union. This makes sense, since we know more about football. The NFL kicks off its regular season next week, as I used to write, and I will not see the first three weekends of games. I may listen to the Vikings on radio. I will buy Monday's papers and read about Sunday's heroes. After we return to New York, I will watch the games and scream at the television set like a great child.

Our magnificent dinner tonight was topped by peach crisp and ice cream. I staggered to the yard. I heard Betty urging the boys to eat more dessert. This is another reason no one ever wants to leave the island.

Our conversation in the yard ended with nightfall and an attack by a holdout squadron of mosquitoes. The moon seemed to be full for about the third night in a row. The moon inspires wonder in these skies.

❖ ❖ ❖ ❖ ❖

We are full circle. I have kept this account for one week, to try to measure time's passage. In a time of doing nothing, it was hard to find time to do this.

I bet that with a few changes, I've been doing what millions of retired people have been doing this past week. The essential joy of it is that I didn't do anything I didn't want to do, except wave "good-bye."

Before me is a *Star Tribune* of July 21, which reports that almost two-thirds of 1,100 adults interviewed for the Minnesota poll said they almost never had idle time. "Even 58 percent of retirees gave that answer."

"Where does the time go?" No one knows.

Labor Day

Mike and Richard left today for North Dakota, Montana, Idaho, and Oregon, where they will visit friends, before pushing on to Los Angeles.

They had been with us a little more than a week, and their departure left a hole in our existence. The company of a bright and cheerful adult who is also your child is irreplaceable. We drove across the lake with the young men and watched them pack Mike's Geo Metro. They are good packers.

Scenes of departure surrounded us at the dock, the Labor Day ritual of good-byes. A portly fellow in a short-sleeved blue shirt hauled his boat from the water and attached it to a trailer. A woman called to her mother about a pile of luggage next to a van. A silver-haired man packed his trunk under the watchful eye of a woman. The other day I saw a child's pail left in the sand outside a shuttered cabin, its blue shadow in the setting sun somehow signaling this season of memory and loss.

The boys drove off. Betty and I shopped. I located a *Star Tribune* with an account of the National Football League's first Sunday. A page-one photograph of a Viking player kneeling in despair was captioned Is It Over Already? Viking fans expect the worst. We ate lunch in a restaurant with a view of the lake and the island, both of them splendid in the glittering sun.

Back on the island, I caught up with an article in yesterday's *Pioneer Press*. It reviewed a book that attacked the perception that labor's insistence on high wages is a basic cause of the nation's trade deficit. I never believed that unions were a basic cause of the economy's recent dismal performance. It is always a pleasure to have my prejudices confirmed.

I live on the fruits of labor and on this day I have no trouble toasting the American worker, having been one so recently myself. In all my years of writing news, I do not recall Labor Day ever being a holiday for me. The thought, as Betty and I swim, is as refreshing as the lake.

Islanders held their annual Labor Day picnic the other day, at a cabin down the line. About forty people attended. Not many were union members—the teachers, certainly, but few others, unless you count the medical and bar associations as unions. We said good-bye to a number of friends at the picnic. The island is now pretty much abandoned to the retired. The only other two occupied cabins in our bay belong to the retired. In the next bay, all the cabins are closed.

We could form our own association of the retired and solicit advice on the art of saying good-bye when we are genuinely sorry to see friends and loved ones leave the island and genuinely happy that we are not.

I was writing in the cabin the other day when I heard Betty on the front porch talking to someone on the path. As I reached the porch, I heard a white-haired fellow, who was accompanied by a woman, ask Betty, "Perhaps you can tell me what happened to the television journalist who lived in this cabin twenty years ago?"

This same couple, visitors at a summer camp, had stopped to chat with us on a July day in 1971 when a messenger from across the lake interrupted us to say CBS was calling me from New York. I boated to a mainland lodge, where the nearest telephone then existed, and was told Louis Armstrong had died and I was wanted to write a special for Walter Cronkite the next day.

The couple seemed surprised to find I was still in the cabin, as though I might have flown off that day to some eternal project. Not long after, I was sitting outside Molly's place when a young camper, passing by, asked me, "Are you the writer for CBS?" I started to answer, "No, I'm the retired guy," but he was only a boy, and I suppose on some level I will always be the writer for CBS, as the plumber is always the plumber.

This Labor Day's chief significance for me has nothing to do with labor. It is just twenty years since I had my most recent drink of alcohol. I do not say "last" because I will not know if it was my last until I draw my last breath. A drunk cannot be too sure of abstinence, as I learned two decades ago.

I had quit drinking the previous February. I had not until then seriously considered quitting, although I should have.

And why did I drink? That is a question Dr. Ruth Fox did not bother to ask. I think I drank to make a good time better. That may sound like a simplification, but if there was a deeper, darker reason, I never learned it.

In AA, I heard people testify that they drank out of fear or a dread without name. An old phrase for liquor was "Dutch courage," and I may have taken a bracer or two, but I did not live with fear as a companion. I heard people say they drank because they were unhappy. I have never been unhappy for more than a brief period, certainly not long enough to get in difficulty with the bottle.

I am a fairly tense fellow, and alcohol offers a release from tension. A drink is welcome at the end of a hard day to many people who are not drunks. Not long after I quit drinking, I faced a tough assignment with long hours, a political convention, I think. I asked Dr. Fox if she could recommend something besides alcohol to relax me. She suggested a long, warm bath. She was right.

As I said, I think I started drinking to make a good time better. After I crossed the undiscovered line into alcoholism, I drank medicinally, to keep going.

Betty and I, at Dr. Fox's recommendation, attended a series of lectures by a professor who was a recovering alcoholic. He said he often spoke to junior high school students. He said that when he asked the students to list occasions when it was acceptable to get drunk, the boys always chose happy times—celebrating victory after a big game, being promoted—and the girls always chose sad times—the death of a parent, the breakup of a romance. He said this gender difference was invariable.

Drunks' stories are the same, and each is different. They are the same because they center on people with a common disability. Drunks are addicted to alcohol. The drug that colonial Americans called "the good creature of God" becomes Cassio's "enemy" that "men put in their mouths to steal away their brains." The specifics of the story vary.

I started drinking beer by the volume my junior year in high school. A group of us held twice-weekly beer parties, stag on Wednesdays, with rotating hosts, and coed on Saturdays, when we met in the home of a young woman whose parents left the city on weekends. We were middle class and properly raised, but I think we were given loose rein by our parents because this was during World War II, and all our futures were the armed forces. It would have seemed silly, with the world coming to an end, to tell a seventeen-year-old boy not to drink beer. Anzio and the Tarawa were on the radio. I remember Mother coming home in tears one after-noon. She had just learned that the son of one of her best friends had died in the war.

We were too young to drink legally; the drinking age in Wisconsin was twenty-one. But alcohol was a socially sanctioned drug, and Milwaukee was sometimes called "the beer city." We had no trouble buying beer, or finding a tavern with a dance band and an age-blind proprietor. No one I knew used any illegal drugs. We had heard of marijuana and cocaine, perhaps even heroin, but they were outside our experience.

The first time I drank hard liquor, at a New Year's Eve party, I blacked out. I awoke sick and shaken. That should have been warning enough.

I had an extraordinary capacity for beer. It dazzled shipmates in the navy and bartenders in college and in Greewich Village, groups with experience of hard drinkers. That is how I thought of myself—as a hard drinker.

I don't think many alcoholics are unaware for a long time that they have a problem, no matter what the drunk tells other people, no matter what he tells himself: he mixed his drinks; he was tired; he was under a lot of pressure. He consoles himself, but beyond equivocation, a merciless truth whispers.

I didn't beat my wife or our children. I didn't raise my voice. I didn't get fired. I functioned. I think most drunks function, although I do not doubt that alcohol causes more damage than all the so-called hard drugs.

One problem with alcoholism is defining it. Doctors now recognize alcoholism as a disease. I think of it more as a condition, which may be a matter of semantics. I heard a woman say at a meeting that she never had more than two drinks in her life, but the second always left her paralyzed. I heard an authority say you could drink a quart of whiskey a day and go to bed dizzy at night and *not* be an alcoholic. I certainly had friends who I do not think were alcoholics, who drank even more than I did.

The most helpful definition of alcoholism I know says that you are an alcoholic if drinking interferes with your work or your family life. It sure interfered with mine.

Alcohol interfered when I was late to work because I had trouble getting out of bed or because I stopped for an eye-opener. (What a fraternity that is, the lodge brothers you find at a bar in the morning, determinedly private, putting away just enough to be civil.)

It interfered when I kept an eye on the clock against lunch hour or the chance for a midafternoon break; it interfered when I did sloppy work; it interfered when I nodded off at dinner; it interfered in ways you hear about at any meeting of Alcoholics Anonymous.

Betty worried. She didn't nag, but she worried. If she told me to be careful about my drinking on a particular occasion, I was careful.

In 1969, Betty and I were at Cape Kennedy for the flight of Apollo 11, which became Neil Armstrong's walk on the moon. I was all pumped up. I had seen and written about earlier space launches at the cape, and they were among the great spectacles of my life, like flying over Kilimanjaro in a sunrise, which I also had done. I had written specials on space, and I was pressing to make this the best I could do. I brought Betty down to the cape from the island, because I wanted her to see this unprecedented shot at the moon.

I was not drinking much, not by my old standards. This is one of alcoholism's little tricks. The morning of the launch, I dressed in darkness. I kissed my sleeping wife. I drank enough leftover whiskey to cover the bottom of the glass.

It was blazing hot in the Florida sun. I worked in an air-conditioned newsroom. I was the only writer present. I spent some time in the sun when Betty arrived. She sat in a bleacher section for guests. I returned to the air-conditioning.

A little later, Betty came to the newsroom to cool off. She was chatting with other CBS wives. We were just minutes away from launch when I got a call from the studio. They wanted me to write a few words. I stood up to run to the studio.

My mouth was full of blood. Some people were holding me up, to my left and right. A doctor in a naval uniform said, "I'm quite sure it's not a heart attack." He looked familiar. I meant to ask, "Doc, were you ever on the *Hoggatt Bay?*" but I couldn't talk.

I remember someone saying, "This craft isn't big enough," meaning a helicopter they were trying to put my stretcher in. Then I came to in a helicopter, and Betty was holding my hand. Someone cried, "Look! There he goes!" and I lifted my head and saw Neil Armstrong and Company lift off from Earth just as I did.

I awoke in a darkened room. I ached all over. Betty sat in a far corner of the room. I had tubes stuck in me, and a machine beeped at the foot of my bed. A doctor came into the room and talked with me.

I went back to unconsciousness. I was exhausted, somewhere beyond tired. The doctor returned. He said I was walking in the valley of the shadow. He told me my heart was in arrhythmia. After a time, a day or more, my heart reregulated itself. It would be a couple of years before I stopped surreptitiously taking my pulse.

I spent about a week in the hospital in Orlando. Then I flew to the island to recuperate for the rest of the summer. CBS News was very good about this. The doctor who treated me in Florida suggested in his written evaluation, although not to me, that I had suffered a convulsive seizure due to withdrawal from alcohol.

A sober person would have seen that stop sign. But I was a drunk, careering along. I didn't drink that summer, but back in the world of work, I was back in the world of the two-martini lunch, and how about topping it off with a brandy?

I don't know how I functioned during those years. More important, I don't know how Betty stood it. The clearest sense I have of that time comes from looking at a copy of the talk Betty gave before an AA-Alanon group in 1974, three years after I quit drinking.

I drank for years, she recalled, before she saw it as a problem. She wouldn't even call it "alcoholism," just a "problem." She accepted whatever rationalization I offered. As the drinking progressed, she recalled, we became more isolated. She became so preoccupied with my drinking that at times it was literally impossible for her to hear our children. "I would find myself asking, 'What did you just say?' " She found herself not talking to people, often in her preoccupation not seeing them on the street.

Alcoholism is a family disease, and the drunk may be the family member who suffers least. Betty thought we were protecting the children, denying there was a problem. But Mike, our seven-year-old, sometimes asked her if there was something wrong. She smiled and said, "No. Everything is just fine." That was a lie, and so was the smile, and he knew it.

Andrew, at age nine, worked his way through page after page in his math workbook, asking the teacher for more problems at recess time.

"Anxiety," Betty said, was pervasive. "My anxiety, not my husband's." For while she rode a roller coaster of moods, "insanely elated" during my times of sobriety, "equally depressed" when I drank, the children continued to be close to me. "He was always kind and could almost always make them laugh," Betty said. "There were times I resented the laughter. If he was drinking, there was no way I could share it, and in my view there was nothing to laugh about."

By this time I was using alcohol as a prescription drug. So much to get through the day, increase dosage as warranted. I don't think I much liked drinking anymore, but as long as I had a medicinal drink I felt fine. I woke in the middle of the night and had a drink. I drank before breakfast. I didn't worry about this. What I thought about at these times was not my family or what I was doing to myself. I thought about whatever I happened to be reading or what the big, irritating news story of the day was.

One night I surprised Betty by calling a friend of ours, an Episcopal priest. He came over to the house and we sat around into the early hours of the morning talking about my drinking, over a drink. I continued drinking. Betty says she became compulsive, insisting the children do their chores a certain way. She suffered anxiety dreams. She pushed herself, rushed. She wanted to control the children's lives. She even tried to control our dreadful, disobedient dog.

The drinking just got worse after my seizure at the cape. One day, Betty turned to a friend for advice, and got me to call AA for the first time. A married couple, both recovering alcoholics, took Betty and me to my first AA meeting. Betty went to Alanon.

"I can't say exactly what the AA meeting did for my husband. He wasn't in very good shape," Betty later told her AA-Alanon audience, "but I will never forget those first hours in Alanon. Here were people who were sane, apparently relaxed, even laughing. There was no smugness or self-pity or desperation."

Alanon was helping Betty before I was able to let AA help me. I quit CBS in the fall of 1970. I needed to make more money. As a first step I got to working on a book. I had all but finished it and was putting the final touches on an introduction when I got so drunk I could not write my name. I finally had had it. This is when a drunk quits drinking—not when his wife has had it, or his children, or his friends, or his colleagues, or his employer. When *he* has had it. I told Betty I was going to call AA again and this time ask for a doctor. She said this was the best news she had had in a long time. Among the names was that of Dr. Ruth Fox. I remembered her as a guest on a program I had written about alcoholism. I called Dr. Fox, and she checked me into a hospital. It took me a few tall drinks to get there.

I was alone in a hospital room. I was really scared. The thought of no liquor scared me. I was beginning to feel the horrors of withdrawal. A nurse gave me a couple of hypodermic shots, vitamins and an anticonvulsant.

Dr. Fox entered the room. She was a short, gray-haired woman. My memory is that she wore a cape, like Margaret Mead, and carried a staff. She sat at the edge of the bed. She asked me how I felt. We chatted.

Then she said, matter-of-factly, "John, you must remember from now on, above all else, that you must never again take a drink of alcohol."

It seemed so obvious, something like revelation. Doctors and others had hinted at this revealed truth. (One doctor wrecked it all by quoting Billy Sunday.) Dr. Fox convinced me. Perhaps I was ready for the message. I don't want to cheapen this by hinting there was anything spiritual in the recognition: no breeze blew. I just believed Dr. Fox knew what she was talking about.

Dr. Fox drew a diagram that showed me what alcohol did to me because I am an alcoholic. She told me I was in for a hideous twenty-four hours. It would be worse than withdrawal from heroin, she said. She said that after twenty-four hours, the alcohol would be out of my system. I would feel weak, but the terrors would be gone. She was right about everything.

In the next twenty-four hours, I learned what "climbing the walls" means. I could only feel, not think. My mind just quit working. There was no such thing as sleep, no comfort. I was shaking and sweaty and cold. I couldn't hold a thought, repeating my name as though it were a mantra, a validation. I couldn't blank out whatever it was that kept me awake.

At the end of the time, the horrors disappeared. I felt as though I were getting over the flu. Dr. Fox returned to tell me she thought my life would be fine, if I just gave up alcohol. She thought I was "psychologically well centered," the only specific words of hers I remember. If I had problems, she said, she was a psychoanalyst and could help me, although she did not think it would come to that.

She wanted me to attend AA meetings again. She said there were more than ninety chapters in the metropolitan area, so I was sure to find a congenial group. She had wide experience with newspaper drunks, and she wanted me to take Antabuse, a drug that does absolutely nothing except make you violently ill if you drink alcohol. She conceded a lot of people didn't approve of Antabuse, but she believed news people are curious by habit and Antabuse prevents them from being curious about what will happen if they take a drink.

I soon found an AA branch I was comfortable with. In the same handsome old church, Betty attended Alanon meetings. Dr. Fox said you learn so many useful things at AA and Alanon meetings that it is a shame you had to be an alcoholic or involved with an alcoholic to attend.

I learned that there is no problem so bad that a good stiff drink will not make worse. I learned that if I needed a drink to enjoy a party I was at the wrong party. I learned the worth of patience and tolerance. People showed up at AA meetings, as I once had, bowlegged drunk. No one criticized them. One night a well-dressed woman of a certain age, carrying two loathsome little dogs, cried out in the middle of a meeting, "My God! You mean you can't drink *anything*?" She then asked if anyone knew of an organization called "Light Drinkers Anonymous."

I found the meetings full of interest. Drunks ultimately are bores, but they often convey a sense of adventure. No one knows what is coming next. A little lightning storm attends such drunks. They frequently do funny or daring things before the inevitable disaster and humiliation. They talk about this candidly at AA meetings.

I heard people admit they had run through fortunes, destroying families and businesses. They did not want sympathy. They were trying to help their listeners understand things about the powerful drug we were all addicted to. I heard a fellow recall how he emerged from the old Astor bar and saw the big Camel cigarettes billboard across the way and the next thing he knew he was in Cairo, with no recollection of how he got there.

I heard a man say he once asked a big Texan how long he had been a member of AA and the Texan replied, "Twenty-five years." "Twenty-five *years*?" exclaimed the questioner. "That's a long time without a drink." "I didn't say I didn't have a drink," the Texan roared. "I said I been going to AA for twenty-five years."

I heard a woman in real estate say she got so she thought

nothing of showing clients around properties while she wore a nightgown and carried a martini. (I knew all about this. I once insisted an executive join Betty and me at our home for dinner and greeted him while I was in my pajamas.)

I learned that alcoholics do not get time off for good behavior. That is, if a drunk quits drinking alcohol for a time, five months or five years, he is not going to be twenty years old again. If he takes another drink, he will be right back where he was when he had his last drink, a bag of wet laundry.

I accepted that knowledge in my head, but not in my heart. I worked that spring of 1971 on a sports magazine proposed for television. A sponsor bought it. (A year later, the show was sold to CBS Sports, and I was back working for the Network with a Heart.) I spent that summer on the island, commuting to New York for the Louis Armstrong special and work on the magazine show. I was on top of the hill.

Toward summer's end, I quit taking Antabuse. I was called back to New York to write the script for the first sports magazine broadcast. The stewardess offered me a martini. Why not? I thought. With everything going so well, why not?

In less than a week, I was back in the hospital. I had been sitting in the apartment, smashed. Betty, on the island with the children, could not reach me. The producer of the sports show could not budge me. It took friends I had known and loved almost as long as I had known and loved Betty to finally get me to call Dr. Fox.

Dr. Fox sounded neither surprised nor disappointed.

I did not have the horrors this time because the alcohol had felled me so quickly. I felt worse emotionally than I did the first time I was hospitalized by drink. I had let everyone down—Betty, the children, Dr. Fox, the people I worked with. Dr. Fox was not exactly cheerful when she came to see me, but she was not condemnatory. She said a slip was quite common. She said there wouldn't be a second slip.

So far, twenty years this Labor Day weekend, there hasn't been.

❖ ❖ ❖ ❖ ❖

It is easier to be a recovering alcoholic in the 1990s than it was in the 1970s. People are no longer surprised when I turn down a cocktail or when I don't drink wine with my meal. A lot of people who are not alcoholics are in self-imposed health programs that preclude alcohol. Young people I know seem to do more running these days than drinking.

The biggest change I have seen in journalism, bigger than satellites or the weather map, is that there is so much less drinking and smoking. After the broadcast, or the final edition, we headed for a saloon to go over the day. There were news people who didn't drink or smoke, but none that I hung out with.

City rooms and newsrooms used to be hazy with cigarette smoke. By the time I retired, smoking was banned in the newsroom, an event as unthinkable as the death of communism in the Soviet Union.

I am not embarrassed by my alcoholism. Even in sobriety I am not perfect. I don't talk much about alcoholism because, as a subject, it seems to me to be about as interesting as a head cold. I was taught that the proper answer to the question "How do you feel?" is "Fine." Mother said, "No one wants to hear an organ recital."

I never say I am an alcoholic unless circumstances force me to because I am afraid that people will read more into it than is there, think my story is somehow dramatic. We are not talking *de profundis.*

People with drinking problems, hearing that I no longer drink, sometimes come to me for advice. There is not much I can tell them except to quit drinking and not to take any drug designed to make them feel better. I tell them better people than I am have not been able to quit, but my experience is that quitting alcohol need not be an agony. For me abstinence certainly beats moderation.

It was much easier for me to stop drinking than it was to stop smoking cigarettes. Now nicotine, there's a drug that beats alcohol all hollow for addiction. I stopped smoking cig-arettes and the nicotine, unlike alcohol, did not flee my system in twenty-four hours. I was sick and giddy for weeks, nau-seated, jumpy, and thick tongued. Food lost its taste. And it was years before I stopped missing a cigarette in the morning or after making love or after a meal or while I was writing.

Betty and I agree that both of us came out of my struggle with alcohol stronger people than we had been. As it is a family sickness, it is a family fight to beat the addiction. Betty and I overcame something tough together, and it gave us a strength that has seemed to put life in perspective.

One thing I learned from Alcoholics Anonymous has nothing to do with drinking. I learned just how well an or-ganization can work. I know drunks who say they cannot attend AA meetings because they cannot stand "all that reli-gious stuff." In my group this consisted of saying the Lord's Prayer, if you were so inclined. You could also keep your mouth shut, but I think that people who have trouble with the Lord's Prayer do not understand poetry, or perhaps they are not ready to get sober.

There also are drunks who say they cannot believe in a Higher Power (in capitals). I think just about everyone ac-knowledges a higher power, whether it is God or pure reason, Mammon or baseball, something that is more important than the individual.

A few years after I quit drinking I realized I no longer feared death. I mean that literally. My grandmother died a long death from cancer in the building where I lived as a youngster, and my uncle died in a fall not long after, and I recall a Victorian photograph of some ancestor, a boy in a velvet jacket in a coffin, some distant ancestor, and I think all of this might have spooked me. I saw a fair amount of death in the navy. For whatever reason, the idea of death scared me.

I nearly died when I suffered the seizure at the cape. I learned that death is no great thing. If death is the soft sense of unutterable fatigue, easing into nothingness, there is noth-ing to scare me.

I will not be happy to leave this world. I am having a wonderful time, and my experience this first retirement year is that the sweetness of life keeps getting sweeter. If I live just four more years, I will have lived longer than either of my parents, either of my sisters, any of my four uncles, and all but one of my grandparents. It is a goal I hope to achieve, but I am aware that I may not, and I am not burdened by the thought. I think much less about death as I approach it than I did when I was a young man. I don't avoid the thought. I am just not interested.

I learned another thing in recovering from alcoholism. All my life, people have been telling me they would like to keep up with the news, but they are just too busy to read the newspapers. It seems necessary for them to make this confession.

Well, I never knew anyone busier than Dr. Ruth Fox, as you can imagine, looking after newspaper drunks. Dr. Fox knew all about the latest news, not just the world and national events, but books and what was at the movies.

I asked her how she kept informed. She said she looked through the *Times* each morning and tore out articles she wanted to read. She stowed these clips in her pockets and purse and during those minutes of the day when she waited for a cab or an elevator or for lunch, she read the stories. She said she saved Russell Baker for the last, or else it seemed as though he had written everything.

I think about Dr. Fox from time to time. One of the things retired people are warned against is drinking. Extra time, boredom, loss of prestige, health worries—all these, we are told, can lead older people to the bottle. I think I will find better things to do. I was told I would. Dr. Fox is one of my higher powers.

What I Was

"On March 31, Doll Rafferty, 135½, substituting for the ailing Juste Fontaine, showed what kind of foe Fontaine would have faced when he spent three rounds 'dressing up' Joe Rivera of Puerto Rico, and then finished him in the fourth."

So ran the lead to "In Milwaukee Rings" by John Mosedale, which appeared in the June 1944 issue of *The Ring* magazine. I was a senior in high school, and I had been Milwaukee correspondent for Boxing's Bible for most of the year. I gave up the column when I went into the navy in June.

Like the old suitor who, going through the attic, rereads his love's billets-doux, I am engaged in a walk through my past to discover the youth who fathered the man. It is a retirement job, for a fellow with plenty of time.

My writing, gratis, for *The Ring* was my first appearance in print outside of school publications. I must have been a novelty among the magazine's correspondents, many of whom were managers and publicists, pushing their interests. I was only a school boy, so unconnected I paid my own way into the arena.

My predecessor on the job was Pinkey Mitchell, younger brother of Richie Mitchell, who gave me boxing lessons at my Uncle Walt's request and who, more famously, almost beat the great Benny Leonard in the old, old Madison Square Garden in 1921. The bout was sponsored by Miss Anne Morgan, of the House of Morgan, for French war relief and was purportedly the first fight attended by a large number of society people. "I never seed anything like it," said the promoter.

I was a young correspondent, but I showed promise as an expert, in case I decided not to try reporting. My column ended, under the heading of "Between Rounds," with a confident metaphor: "Word is that Milwaukee will soon be invaded by an influx of New York managers and fighters. The heavy sugar is drawing flies." My only source for the "word" would have been my tough little Scottie Hank, but I tossed off this view of the future with the confidence of an authority on the Soviet Union, or an economist.

I was extremely proud to write for *The Ring*. I started reading the magazine when I was nine, and I didn't stop until I was nearing thirty, after the Sweet Science had lost its way.

We have a box of *Rings* from the 1930s and '40s in the cabin and a couple of boxes in New York. I have not looked at them for years, but now that I am retired, I turn to the issue of September 1949 and find an article by the president of the Shakespeare Club of New York, which in 1991 is not listed in the telephone directory, so debased are the times we live in. Arthur Heine assembled quotes from the works which might apply to the Manly Art: "Do you not see that I am out of breath?" (*Romeo and Juliet*); "We must have bloody noses and crack'd crowns" (1 *Henry IV*); "Knock him down there" (2 *Henry VI*) and so on.

In my line, the uses of algebra were transient, but *The Ring* provided interest that stuck to the ribs. Here on the cover of the issue for June 1953 is Charles Humez, a French middleweight. Three years later, I took Betty, early in our courtship, to see Humez fight Ralph "Tiger" Jones in the old Garden. Betty called the French embassy for pointers. "A bas! A bas!" she cheered. "Hit him in the belly!" I cheered.

Near *The Ring* in the storage space are copies of my high school magazine, *Mercury,* which I served at various times as short story writer, poet, sports editor, cartoonist, and illustrator. It may be better not to look back, but it is unavoidable. *Mercury* was a handsome publication, about thirty glossy pages a copy, issued four times a school year.

I can recover none of my poetry. God is good. I was a blank verse man. I find myself represented as a freshman by a story called "World's Chump." It begins, "Matt French shifted nervously in the ring and kept his eyes glued on the floor. Matt never looked at the man he was about to fight . . . ." and goes on to tell how Matt, a champion, gives up the ring for a singing career. He fails embarrassingly and returns to *le boxe,* wiser. I had just seen *Citizen Kane.*

The stories march through my high school career. They are frankly derivative. "Worthington Twiddle twaddled home" and learned the true meaning of the season in "A Christmas Carol—1943." "One Must Win" is a lady-or-the-tiger story about a prize fight; "The Macbeths of Sumner Street" is a murder mystery which begins, "I had been with the Macbeths about three weeks when old Duncan came to visit. . . ."

Mercury offers evidence that I even then was in the presence of better writers than I was. This didn't bother me. I was in love with writing, and I wrote for the pleasure of it. My idea of a really good writer was Shakespeare. After that, comparisons were odious.

Mercury carried humor. HE: Whatever became of those old-fashioned girls who fainted when a boy kissed them? SHE:

Whatever became of those old-fashioned boys who made them faint? A 1943 joke.

There is much in the magazine about academic excellence, much about school sports, proms, Sadie Hawkins dances, to which girls invited boys, and pigtail days. We were adolescents, swollen by tumult and confusion, and any official publication is best foot forward, but *Mercury* reminds me how much fun it was to be a high school student in those days right after the Great Depression and during the bloodiest war in history.

Meanwhile, I produced a boxing magazine called *Leather Week* for an audience of none. I am sure I did not read it once it was composed. My mother or my sisters would have had no interest in *Leather Week*. I didn't show it to friends. But each Wednesday night during my sophomore year, I sat down and cartooned and wrote about boxing around the world as harvested, or swiped, from the sports pages, augmented with feature stories drawn from memory.

Leather Week is penciled, four to six pages long. It must have taken hours to produce. I can't imagine how I got my homework done on Wednesdays. This was the year of plane geometry. How did I survive?

I loved baseball and football and improved my hours and my intellect by reading about them, but it is boxing that I wrote about. Why did I write this diary of the seedy sport, devote hours of adolescence to composing, in effect, letters to myself? What possessed me?

I even kept up with *Leather Week* that summer when I was breathless in love, dazed by the thought of a girl no older than Virginia Clemm. Her touch made my kneecaps jump. But I cranked out my boxing magazine, asking her to report on radio coverage of a fight when I was otherwise occupied. ("Bobby 'Blue Eyes' Ruffin," she began her notes.)

I think the only answer to my compulsive production is that a writer writes. I might miss a homework assignment or cut a class, but I never missed the Wednesday night deadline I imposed on myself for *Leather Week*.

Before *Leather Week*, there was *Abdul, Crime Destroyer*.

171

Abdul had an audience, chiefly high school beaus of my sister's undoubtedly eager to please her. There were forty-six *Abdul* adventures, about twelve handwritten pages each, with illustrations. An aunt had given me a rubber stamp set, and I used the stamps for the title page and the initial letter of story sections, and I suppose it was having the stamp set that inspired me to follow Conan Doyle. The story titles gave away the plot. "An Agent in Trouble," Volume Four. "The Subamarine [*sic*] of Death," Volume Ten. "The Kidnapers [*sic*]," Volume Sixteen.

Looking back on this output of my youth, I find the published writing to be callow, although it must have had comparative merit to have been chosen for the school magazine. I am impressed by *Abdul* and, even more, by *Leather Week*, which seem products of a born reporter, so anxious to set it down, to tell a story, that he will report the story if only to himself. The work is the product of an impulse that is almost an instinct.

Mother also saved panels from a giant work a friend and I planned, showing an all-out brawl in what appears to be a five-storey hotel and bar. The *oeuvre* was intended to cover the pump room table. Men are punched, kicked, garrotted, and clubbed, gang-tackled and felled by falling anvils. They are even shot, although knuckles and knives were the preferred weapons in those less murderous times.

Mother also saved, in an imitation leather binding, *Billy and Betty and Tag Their Dog Out West*, a 231-page novel in erractic scrawl, written when I was eight. My first heroine was named "Betty."

❖ ❖ ❖ ❖ ❖

All telephone calls are business calls. Letters are for intimacy. Betty and I come from families that expected letters. If you were away, you wrote. We have stacks of letters we have written each other. They are the account of our life together. They are priceless to us; of no value to anyone else.

When I was in the navy, my first time away from home,

I regularly wrote my mother, my sisters, a love interest, high school friends, and old shipmates. My family later told me how they appreciated my letters because they generally were cheerful. I wish this showed strength of character on my part, but the fact is I enjoyed navy life. I disliked boot camp and I wasn't crazy about San Diego, where I attended hospital corps school, but once I reached the Bay area and later picked up a ship, I was as happy as Barnacle Bill. Or so I remembered it.

I was a wildly romantic young man. I was Romeo, Frederick Henry, Gatsby. I was ready to keel for my woman. I filled spiral notebooks with foolish love stories. World War II encouraged that sort of thing. Longing and loss were in the air. The end of everything seemed implicit in the beginning.

I am looking at letters I wrote my mother from the USS *Hoggatt Bay CVE 75*. I shipped out in early November 1945.

"They had us on the flight deck, and as we went under the Golden Gate Bridge (at 0930), some little private yacht tooted madly, and drunken men and women waved their bottles at us." I reported I was unsteady but never seasick.

There are the obligatory complaints. ("Our orders, as usual, have been changed, and we're going to Okinawa instead of New Caledonia.")

The sailor is a youth and rebounds: " . . . watched the sunset at sea tonight, and it was beautiful and there's a peace out here. . . . I was sitting on the sponson and the sky was halved by afterglow at the bow and dusk aft."

But also, "At the beginning of this week I suffered the world's worst depression . . . and I'm glad I'm out of it. I worked it out by going to the heavy bag, and I forgot to take my rings off. I shredded the skin on my knuckles and strained my left duke so it was useless. . . . I had the duty and spilled the sick bay's chow down the ladder."

Through my two years in the navy I used Schlitz as a symbol of freedom. My references to women were bowdlerized and suitable for network radio. I "danced to Stan Kenton at the San Diego Palladium until 2 A.M. . . ." " . . . danced to Charley Barnett at the Los Angeles Palladium until 2 A.M." I did not discuss my partners, who I remember as defense plant workers and high school girls. I refer to "Japs." I call land duty "woman's work." I write that I need "a blonde and a bottle of Schlitz."

I demanded mail. Saipan and Guam and Okinawa, recently purchased with blood, were mail drops to me, as were San Francisco, Los Angeles, Jacksonville, and Boston.

"Dribbles of mail," I lament. "Most of it is supposedly at Guam. SNAFU! Got one letter from you, and one from Dote and [the love interest] and Aunt Doie and Father Stimpson. . . . "

The sailor is a long time removed from the retired gent who is reading over his shoulder, but in some ways he is the same fellow. On April 8, 1946, I wrote: "If it is possible to fall in love with a city, I have done it. I now know there is no other place in the world like New York, that other so-called 'big towns' are merely imitations of THE big town."

A couple of shipmates and I had come down from Boston for a weekend. It was the first time any of us had seen New York. I was enthusiastic about everything, beginning with the train which offered "very clean, air-conditioned cars and courteous service."

We took a room at the Taft, "for two dollars and something apiece." I placed the hotel "just off Fifth." We drank a beer in the "Taproom at the Taft—Vincent Lopez was there." (Just as Vincent Lopez, his tinkling piano, and his orchestra would be there a decade later, for Betty and me to dance to as newlyweds.)

My shipmates and I dined at Jack Dempsey's ("quite a collection of pugs"); we walked down "the Great White Way" to Times Square, stopping at the Latin Quarter for "an excellent review, beautiful showgirls and a couple of comedians." (And Ann Corio tossed her bra into the audience at the blackout.)

We patronized Eddie Condon's in the Village, the high point of the trip. I listed the jazz folk present, the songs they played and sang. ("Bud Freeman dropped in for a few numbers.") We stayed until 2:30. We rose at noon on Sunday, leisurely as any admiral, and ate brunch at Rockefeller Center. I admired the ice skaters and "the tulips and hyacinths." Did I know a hyacinth from a battleship? I must have gotten my hands on a brochure.

We visited the top of the RCA building, "70 storeys—it was clear and sunny and crisp—Brooklyn and the George Washington bridge, the Chrysler building, St. Patrick's Cathedral etc." In 1946 these all were national monuments.

My shipmates and I toured the NBC studios. "We watched *The National Hour* with Robert St. John and got the dope on all the workings. They 'televised' Robbie for us—really an amazing thing to see. He was so startled he could hardly speak."

We visited the Museum of Modern Art. I didn't think much of a South Seas exhibit, but I liked "Cezanne, Van Gogh, Epstein, Miro and Dali." I loved Renoir's *Little Margaret Barard*. We took a bus "up to Washington Square." I literally did not know up from down. But by the time we boarded the 12:30 A.M. to Boston, I was hooked. "Lord, how I hated to leave that wonderful town," I wrote, "but there will be other New York liberties."

It is easy to patronize ourselves as youth, but the retired gent understands the sailor. A few weeks after that first trip, I visited New York alone and this time saw *Showboat* and dined in the Ziegfeld restaurant where a kind waiter pointed out Miss Carol Bruce drinking a martini at the bar before she broke my heart singing "Bill" and "Can't Help Lovin' That Man." In the lobby, I bought the cast album. The next day while waiting for a sightseeing bus in mid-Manhattan, I saw my first television event, Charley Keller hitting a home run to defeat Cleveland way uptown in the Bronx. I bought Mother a framed reproduction of the Renoir, and Little Margaret now smiles over Betty and me as we sleep in New York.

I returned to the Hub, where we were putting the *Hoggatt Bay* in mothballs. I was discharged in a couple of months. The twenty-year-old sailor standing on a Boston street, baffled, angry, and happy, is what I was, not exactly what I became. It would take seven years to get there, but I already was a citizen of New York.

❖ ❖ ❖ ❖ ❖

Frank Sinatra holds no particular meaning for Betty, but he is the great saloon-singer of my lifetime and just three of the songs on a tape—"I Didn't Sleep a Wink Last Night," "Five Minutes More," and "Put Your Dreams Away"— placed me, respectively, in high school, the navy, and college. I have been listening to Sinatra since my sister urged him on me in the 1940s. Upwards of six decades. It is as though in the 1940s I listened to a popular singer who first became famous in the 1880s.

The Sinatra stayed in my head today as Betty and I swam and read and ate dinner and visited neighbors. I went to sleep hearing the songs of my youth. I woke up around 1:30 this morning, to the sounds of heavy rain.

I padded into the living room and did something I have been meaning to do for decades, a perfect retirement occupation. I went through the piles of 78-rpm records stored in the painted orange crate in a corner of the living room. They are as much a part of this summer place as the knotholes in the ceiling.

A friend in New York assured me there is a big market for old 78s. He suggested I clean the records up and bring them east. This is far too cagey for me. I look at the labels and often not just the song but the arrangement comes back to me. Our memory for matter learned in youth seems bottomless.

I played some of the records, the volume turned to a whisper in the rainy night, so as not to disturb Betty. These are the bands of Goodman, Tommy Dorsey, Jimmy Dorsey, Miller, Krupa, Bob Crosby, Herman. Sinatra sings "Stardust" with Jo Stafford and the Pied Pipers for T. Dorsey. Bob Eberle and Helen O'Connell sing "Green Eyes" for J. Dorsey. I play "Don't Cry, Baby" by Erskine Hawkins, the Twentieth-Century Gabriel.

It is three o'clock. I return to bed. I awake still a creature of the past. After breakfast, I return to the records.

Older-timers than I lament the passage of the parlor piano and folk gathered around for a sing. I am not much on community song. I listen to these records and the summers of my youth return, my sisters are girls in halters and shorts, my mother is offering us iced tea in the depression heat and Cab Calloway is singing "It Ain't Necessarily So."

Jo Stafford sings "Long Ago and Far Away." ("Long Afar and Go Away," sang the sweet girls of high school, clouded in gardenia perfume.) I play Lee Wiley's "Someone to Watch Over Me," my favorite recording of that great song. I play Frances Langford's lachrymose "Then You've Never Been Blue" and Perry Como's "If You Were the Only Girl in the World." I play records Bing Crosby made in the 1930s and Maxine Sullivan's "Ev'ry Time We Say Good-bye" with Teddy Wilson on the piano.

"Goodness, they were romantic," Betty says, looking up from the desk where she is dealing with the reality of checks and bills.

We dance, an old party and his younger wife in a cabin on an island in a late summer rain. We jitterbug in a postage stamp of space to Dick Stabile's "Just Because" and J. Dorsey's "Long John Silver," dance until we are winded by music that was written and recorded before either of us knew the other lived.

The Edge of Sadness
Friday, September 20

An edge of sadness threatens Betty and me. It is the knowledge that we leave the island on Thursday.

"Let's stay through the harvest moon," I said last month.
The full moon and the autumn equinox fall on Monday, and
we will tack on a couple of days. I felt cocky. Retirement
meant that we could base important decisions on whims.

Our whims are limited because Betty must get back to
her teaching. A recent mail brought a letter from the mother
of one of Betty's former students. The letter was full of love
and gratitude for what Betty had done for the student. When
we return to the city is of no importance to me, but it will

mean a great deal to some young people in need of help.

Now Betty and I are experiencing the jumpy, irrational behavior we noticed affecting friends earlier in the summer. Leaving the island troubles islanders. The weather remains chilly and damp. Betty hopes it will clear so that she can paint the back stoop. I spent the morning at this computer.

We took a load of trash to the recycling bin on the mainland. What we don't recycle we burn. What we don't burn we dump in our garbage pit. We mailed letters, picked up mail and our newspapers.

Back on the island, I looked over the *Times* of last Sunday. A REMEDY FOR OLD RACISM HAS NEW KIND OF SHACKLES, said the *Times*. FABLED FOR DETAILS, CIA NOMINEE FACES QUESTIONS ON FORGETFULNESS, said the *Times*. TEEN-AGER FOUND CHAINED IN BRONX, GUNS 'N' ROSES AGAINST THE (EXPLETIVE) WORLD, says the *Times*.

Do we really want to go back to where that stuff is important?

A FED-UP BUSH WARNS IRAQ, says the *Star Tribune*. AMERICAN POOR STAY POOR LONGER, GET LESS HELP THAN CANADA OR WESTERN EUROPE, says the *Grand Forks Herald*.

Of course it is important to know these things, to be informed citizens of this ghastly century. We cannot spend the rest of our lives hand in hand in the piney woods, Betty and I, watching the play of red leaf and yellow, studying the skunk and the flight of the eagle.

But really, who wants to return to the sleazy sideshows in Washington, the malevolent struggles in the Middle East, the ludicrous rivalries of Eastern Europe and the former Soviet Union; who wants to listen to the socio-babble and the politi-babble and the eco-babble?

I am in no position to carry on like a sophomore who has just learned that life is hard. I am enjoying my personal definition of the best of life, and the world I am returning to promises adventure.

On my desk is a letter from a friend at CBS Sports. He tells me he wants me to write for Sports's coverage of the Olympic winter games in the Alps next February. It frightens me to think how much of the good part of life results from coincidence. Betty and I were walking onto a dance floor last December at a party for Walter Cronkite when my friend from Sports was leaving the floor. He asked me, in passing, what I was up to, and I said I was about to retire. "Why don't you come and write the Olympics for us?" he asked.

"How would you like to come to the Alps with me?" I murmured in Betty's ear as we danced. "Then we could go to Venice for a few days and blow the fee." She smiled and yes, she said yes.

I had dropped my friend a line earlier this summer expressing my interest and giving him our island address in case he wanted to get in touch with me. Now here was the offer, on a piece of paper. It had all seemed a dizzy and romantic interlude, fancy. Now it is as real as jury duty.

Over the top of this computer, through the window of our sons' bedroom which I have been using as my study this summer, I look into the green world.

In front of a big fire in the fireplace last night, the wall furnace humming along, I read the Sunday *Times* book review. I read:

"Hume Cronyn calls his memoir *A Terrible Liar*. He has reread a diary he kept during a 1966 safari in Kenya. The diary records episodes of gastritis, influenza, undelivered supplies and anxiety about children. What Cronyn remembers of the safari are snow peaks, desert spaces, animal herds, campfires and the silence of the stars."

I read from a letter of the dying Keats:

> "How astonishingly does the chance of leaving the
> world impress a sense of its natural beauties on us.
> Like poor Falstaff, though I do not babble, I think
> of green fields. I muse with the greatest affection
> on every flower I have known from my infancy—
> their shapes and colors are as new to me as if I had
> just created them with a superhuman fancy."

These optimistic reflections are the products of civilized, you might say urban, sensibilities—an actor, a poet, and they blunt the leading edge of sadness.

Full Moon
Monday, September 23

I am as edgy these days as an adolescent who is not sure his love is returned. I am irritated at my irritation, a man old enough to be retired from gainful employment acting like a schoolboy because it is near time to leave the summer place.

Betty and I walk in the shadow of departure. Walks we take, views we look to, we are walking and seeing for the last time this year. Each step we take draws us closer to our leave-taking; each tick of the clock is numbered. It is ludicrous; I am going back to a life of relaxation in a city I love, and I mourn. I know there is next summer, but there has been a next summer for sixty years and it never seems to ease the pain of *this* summer's end.

Fall officially arrived a little before eight o'clock this morning. We were not awake to welcome it. We struggled out of our warm bed into a living room temperature of about fifty degrees.

The day is sunny, after a week of cloudy skies. The lake is calm after a week of roiling. The trails are scattered with leaves, pine needles, and branches. The weather people assure us clouds will arrive this afternoon and stay to obscure the full moon. If that is the case, Betty and I will stare from the lake at the black sky where the moon should be.

Today is Laura and Matt's second wedding anniversary. They were married under a big tent in Connecticut while the remains of Hurricane Hugo danced attendance. There was a time when Molly wasn't around. I find that hard to believe.

Betty and I had business on the mainland. Our mail includes a jury notice for me. I am expected to report September 30, a week from today. I will not be back in the city by that date. Can I tell the County of New York that we lost island time because of Betty's eye operation and that there is a full moon tonight and that we plan a leisurely drive through parts of Ontario and Quebec?

The jury summons seems symbolic of what we are going back to, the world of the criminal, or at least the accused. That world is here, too. Some islanders' cars were vandalized in their mainland parking spots this summer. One car was torched. The alleged evildoers are a fifteen-year-old and two nine-year-olds; even on the island we must acknowledge crime.

I am a regular juror in New York. I am called every couple of years. It used to be that I was never put on a jury; I could count on reading a Victorian novel during my term of service. An old-timer told me I would never serve because I was a newsman. That changed a decade or more ago. I am told that jury pools are smaller because of budget cuts, and the law in its awful majesty can no longer be fastidious.

I hate jury duty. I hate passing judgment, no matter how

guilty the wretch. It just gets worse. The courtrooms are crummier. Now the jurors as well as the judged must pass through a metal detector. I hate jury duty, and I think I have to do it.

I ask for a delay in a scribbled note to the County of New York on paper borrowed from the drugstore. Betty and I drive twenty miles to a branch of the state university with a sample of our well water for testing. We have never had this done, not in half a century. We want to be sure the water is fit for Molly. What could go wrong down there, 130 feet below the tread of man?

Over a restaurant sandwich, I tell Betty perhaps I could teach a journalism course at the university branch. There is no real need for us to leave this region. We could build a house by the side of the road. We run a couple of errands. We buy tomato cages we hope will keep the deer from eating some pine saplings in our yard.

As we drive back to the island the clear sky of morning is now a field for white lambs. The high school gridders are walking to their practice field when we reach the village. They are younger than any of our children. I see by the paper they are having a tough year. When they play at home on Friday nights, the lights of their football field peer across the lake, above the line of pines, like the giant eyes of Dr. T. J. Eckleburg.

In the world before lights, in 1953 when they played their football in the day, I crossed the lake to see every home game the high school team played. I stood along the sidelines with the other spectators. The team was undefeated and untied. I later stood on the sidelines to watch NFL football in stadiums from New York to Los Angeles and from Green Bay to Dallas. I never felt closer to the game than I did watching the team from the north woods high school.

Betty and I crossed the lake to the island and stored the boat in the shore station belonging to Betty's mother. We removed the motor from the shore station, and I lugged it up the bank. I will operate the lift by hand these last few days. It seemed to me I did this job about two weeks ago. I don't mean carrying the motor down the hill at summer's start; I mean carrying it up at the end of last summer. It was no time ago. Betty cooks dinner. I haul in logs for the fire. We eat as the sun drops behind a pile of purple clouds. Most of the sky is cloudy now, but there is a brilliant afterglow, streaks of yellow and orange along the horizon.

After dinner, we put on thermal underwear and heavy clothes, including wool socks, gloves, and wool caps. We grab seat cushions and paddles, and we go down the hill to our canoe.

The temperature is in the low forties, and it will drop. As we launch the canoe, there are only a few patches of hunter orange afterglow on the horizon. The lake is as still as water in a glass.

We canoe away from the dock. This is what we had in mind all summer, although we did not say it, canoeing under the harvest moon. There may be no moon visible, but we are on the lake.

Although all the cabins on our shore are deserted, the silence is not complete. A couple of fisher folk are trolling along the point, quietly chugging, their small craft lit at both ends so our canoe will not crash into it.

From across the lake, a dog barks. He is not even barking loudly, a kind of halfhearted woofing, but across the flat, quiet lake, his bark might come from a few doors down. We hear a train. We hear the shush of car tires on the mainland highway.

All of that is wrapped in silence.

We can see clouds, which means there are breaks in the cover. We paddle around the point.

Betty spots the moon. She is not sure of what she sees. It looks like ectoplasm, a smudge of grayish white, but it grows brighter until there is no doubt that we are seeing a harvest moon, although I would not want to count on this light to keep working in the fields.

After we paddle a few canoe lengths, the moon seems to change its position in the sky. Now it is out from the clouds. It is not a brilliant moon. There is a ruffle of breeze. We hear one motorboat, and then it is gone. We sit at rest, the paddles across our knees.

The moon is a ghostly galleon, a dead princess, a severed head, the moon is a mystery beyond photography or the description of the learn'd astronomer, and no man has touched it.

The words "night sky" create a fancy of different images. This sky is dark but fretted with darker clouds. Betty hopes to see some stars, but the sky is moonstruck. What looks like a hole in the sky turns out to be a black cloud, no bigger than a handful of reality.

Reality is the world of insurance, of New York juries, the world of the eye doctor. It all seems far removed from this world of the black northern lake, the chill of this September night, and the benison of vast silence.

The world of the lake and canoe, the world of isolation and the harvest moon is real, but the illusion it fosters is false. The reality of this world is that the real world made the illusion possible. We are here because, among other reasons, I worked forty years so that we could be here on a night in September.

The moon is moving toward the black cloud of reality. Betty and I paddle back to the dock.

It is a time so perfect that it is as if an episode in life followed in every detail a splendid dream.

There is one cautionary note, I think, about being with the woman you love in the canoe on the lake in the isolated September night, and that is, after a day of heavy thought, you might burst your heart with joy.

Home to Home

Thursday, September 26

It is easier to pack than it is to think about packing. Activity quiets the apprehensive stomach.

I learned these truths again today, as Betty and I finished closing the cabin, crossed to the mainland, and set out for New York by way of Canada. I seem to have to learn the truths each year.

Closing our cabin is simple compared to closing other summer places I have heard about. We turn a coat hanger rigged forty years ago to drain the pump. We put up shutters. We set down mouse poison. That's about it, as I explained years ago to a CBS colleague. "You're my idol," he told me.

He said it took him a week to close his summer place on the Jersey shore. His place undoubtedly is more elegant than ours.

Betty does the skill jobs in closing the cabin. I do the heavy lifting. She makes a long list of tasks, proving things are more complicated than I have indicated. I burned the trash for the last time. I carried our new trash burner, unused although we bought it in August, to the outhouse. I also put the grill in there. Betty and I carry the canoe up the bank and chain it to a tree behind the woodshed. We place the Sailfish face down on two-by-fours.

The shutters cover screens and windows that are most open to the winter winds. The shutters are warped and splintered. Each year we talk about doing something more efficient, and at the end of each summer, we struggle getting the old shutters back in place. We often do this in the rain, our heads turned up like turkeys.

Our closing was eased this year by the arrival of friends, a husband and wife, a couple of evenings ago. When he and I were boys, back in the 1930s, the last meal of the summer would be eaten at his family cabin or at our cabin, depending on which family was departing the next day.

We revived this pleasant custom last night. Betty and I were down to not very much food, but it was enough for Betty to prepare a quiche and a major dessert called Texas cake. We also had a little wine and beer left. We ate by candlelight and afterward talked by firelight.

We walked out with our guests. The moon now was white, and it painted the landscape white. That was this season's last island night scene, the trails and clearings and trees white in the moonlight, and the path on the waters.

We woke up at six this morning. The temperature must have been in the thirties. I cowered under the blanket while Betty went to the living room to get the wall furnace started. I heard her laugh. She returned and said, "I guess it's time to go. We're out of propane."

After breakfast, we did dishes for the last time this season. It was so cold in the pump room that my hands ached, and

I periodically ran to the bedroom to warm them over the electric heater. We listened to *Bohème* as we performed the routine final tasks.

We carried the luggage to the dock and walked to the next bay to fetch the *Pequod*. The lake was lively. We unzipped the boat, drove to our dock, loaded the boat, crossed the lake, unloaded the boat, loaded the car, looked back at the island for a last time, and headed north just at noon.

It's never so bad once we are under way. We already were looking ahead. We began seeing color almost immediately, although the leaves on the island had only started to turn. A couple of hours from the island, we stopped for lunch at a restaurant overlooking a pleasant lake, and we talked with excitement about our trip, as though the desolation over departure had been a dream.

We drove along the North Shore of Lake Superior. There was sporadic color. The sun spanked off pines and green leaves and the lake. We drove past elaborate lakeside homes outside Duluth; I visualized the young Fitzgerald outside locked gate, looking in.

We rolled into the resort town of Grand Marais near the Canadian border at dusk. It is a former Indian village and fur-trading post, but it is given over to tourists now, and we had difficulty finding a place to stay. Instead of spending the night in the motel moderne we stayed at a turn-of-the-century frame building on the shores of the lake. It reminded me of the wooden hotels in small towns of my youth.

The floors slanted. The steps were uneven. The proprietors acknowledged this in a note saying that in their desire to keep the hotel "comfy," they hoped we would ignore "the occasional roof leak, the now and then plumbing difficulties." We were being weaned from islandness. We ate an unhurried dinner of Lake Superior fish in the dining room.

We chose a tiny room. We heard the lake on the shore. We were away from the island, but we fell asleep with a sense of lake and pine and a presiding wind.

Friday, September 27

Betty and I sat on our bed in the tiny room this morning, watching the sun rise over Lake Superior. The locals see this every day. When Michael lived in a hotel in Superior, he told us about these dawns on the lake, which he could see from his room.

The rising sun bathed the lake and sky an improbable crimson. I am against seeking out natural marvels to gape at. I think they should come with the territory, occur as the traveler passes by; otherwise, it is like borrowing from a dictionary of quotations without having read the original work.

I ate my delicious unhealthy road breakfast. Betty was more restrained. An hour later we were through customs and in the splendor of the Canadian countryside. Grandeur lies to the west, but, heading east, we were caught by color, balsam and the flash of maples, rock outcroppings, and so many lakes we made a joke of it.

At lunch I read a column by the Washington correspondent of the *Chronicle-Journal* of Thunder Bay. He warned Canadian "continentalists" to think twice before pushing for a link with the United States. He cited the casual accounts on one page of the *Washington Post* of local murder and gun violence. Join the United States, he said, and, "You too will be reading, in 10 lines among the truss ads, about bodies dumped by the road, to be picked up like run-over porcupines." He wrote, "American society has lost its compass."

In late afternoon we reach Longlac, the northernmost point on our trip. The nearest community of any size appears to be hours away, so we elect to stop here. We are now 553 miles from the island. The Muzak as we walk into the dining room is "O Sole Mio."

The night clerk is irritated by Canadian taxes. We have been hearing about the latest tax, the GST, or Goods and Service Tax, which we are told is 7 percent on everything except air. After we take our key, the clerk says, "Of course, it's not much better in the States, is it?" I am equivocal. He adds, "We *do* have a health program."

Saturday, September 28

We awake to a snowfall.

The snow is water before it hits the ground, but when I take the bags to the car, I learn it is real snow. The temperature drops while Betty and I eat breakfast, and the snow is sticking to the ground when we take off.

A burly fellow strides toward the coffee shop. He is dressed like a woodsman, and his shoulders slump under their light burden of snow, as if he knows this is it, winter is here this first week of autumn, another long winter.

We are not going to perish in a blizzard, but the snowfall deepens as we drive. It lies magically on the pines. The snow may be a nuisance to the resident, but it is romance to the traveler.

A moose ambles across the road about fifty yards ahead of us. He does not hustle at our approach, nor does he linger. We are enchanted as children. We have been admiring the Moose Crossing signs with their menacing silhouettes.

We listen to the first tape of our trip, *Turandot,* as we drive through Hearst, more than one hundred miles from Longlac, and we have seen fewer cars than we would if we walked a couple of blocks on Central Park West. The thought of Central Park West cheers me, as the thought of a stroll in the woods cheered me a few days ago.

It is a familiar feeling for both of us. When we flew back to New York at vacation's end, the depression lasted until we were at the Minneapolis–St. Paul airport. Then we started thinking of New York and the year ahead and it was hard to remember that we were saddened by departure.

The snow stops. The sun appears. The lakes gleam and wink. The colors of the foliage look like the palette of a careless painter. For much of the drive we listen to *The Remains of the Day,* Kazuo Ishiguro's novel read by Michael York. We had read this brilliant work last year. A friend of Betty's, hearing of her eye injury, sent her the tape.

We eat lunch in a town called Moonbeam. The only eating establishment we find open is called Della Pieta Pizza. Betty drives five hundred miles today. We speed by scenic beauty we would have paused to admire on the way west. Our blood already quickens to a New York beat.

We find a motel in North Bay, a community of 52,000 people on the shores of a lake that covers 330 square miles at an average depth of 15 feet. They should call it Lake Politician.

We dine to the strains of "Arrivederci, Roma." Our last night on the island a visitor said, "Everywhere I look in this cabin, I see Italian opera." Betty and I travel through many zones—time, geography, psychology, emotion—and we travel in a small bathysphere of Italian influences.

Sunday, September 29

We were on the road, driving into the sun, by seven o'clock this morning and reached Ottawa around noon. When we talked about this trip, I envisioned spending a night there. Now there was no time. We drove to the Parliament buildings. The Peace Tower with its carillon is dedicated to the 66,650 Canadians who died in World War I.

"Slinger" noted in today's *Toronto Star* that with the breakup of the Soviet Union and the potential breakup of China, Canada would become the undisputed biggest nation in the world. "If we are No. 1, does that mean we're a super-power?" he asked. "If we're a super-power, what about global obligations and military preparedness? There are schoolyard drug dealers in Colombia with bigger armies than ours. In our last display of military might, the Gulf war, our air force may have shot something down." And mockery may be the best weapon in a world dominated by great fools.

Panic seized us when we came within one hundred kilometers of Montreal. Our AAA guide book to the city offered a bewildering variety of approaches, hotels, and motels. I had been meaning to study this all summer long, but time got away from me. We stopped at a tourist information booth. A helpful young woman gave us the phone number of a bed and breakfast network and, after we made a reservation, showed us how to find the place.

Smarter than any bomb, Betty navigated the streets of the lovely city. We were a couple of blocks from McGill University in a house and on a street that might have been in Greenwich Village.

I had my New York guard up. I asked our host were the streets around the house safe, was the park at the end of the block safe, was the Metro safe, was Vieux Montreal safe? Betty and I strolled to a charming mall and dined at Vespucci's, which had been recommended by our host, along with Vivaldi's. I asked Betty, "Are you and I the only people on the continent with no Italian blood?"

We crossed the park and took the Metro to old Montreal and walked its handsome streets in the night. As we went to bed, I thought, I hate asking all these questions about safety. I hate the idea of becoming a fearful old man. But we are not on the island. We are heading back to American civilization, as it stands at the end of the twentieth century.

Sunday, September 30

One thing Betty and I agreed on all summer long was that we would spend the final night on the road some place a short drive from New York, so that we would arrive in the city the next morning fresh and alert, prepared to sort through mail, lay in food, take clothes to the dry cleaners, and find other unavoidable ways to spend time and money.

But we got started this morning as though we were on deadline. We allowed ourselves one long look at the great city from Mount Royal, and then we were on what was clearly the home stretch. By the time we saw our first "New York" sign a few miles out of Montreal, I knew that we would spend the night in our apartment and not in Bosky-Beddes-on-the-Hudson.

The skies were overcast as we crossed into the United States. The colors were subdued. Fall will visit, but its approach seemed tentative after the recent show we had seen of snow and flame.

Darkness dropped in as we drove toward Big Town, the jury, the eye doctor, children in need of schooling, hard truths. We paused for gas at a dispiriting service station, a soulless, dun, multi-islanded truck stop with greasy hot dogs and guys standing around with killer eyes and not much to do. I was about to suggest we return to the island.

And then young Fred Astaire briefly bounded into our lives. The young fellow vaulted out of the gloom, his heart full of Ginger, leaping the service islands as if they were low hurdles. He all but sang to us, "What can I do for you folks?"

He filled 'er up. He took Betty's twenty and bounded back to the office for change. "That young fellow is in love," I said to Betty. He returned with our change, warbled a farewell, and, with a move I hadn't seen since Astaire danced with the mop, leaped away to another customer.

It was at that moment I realized how happy I was to be home, how unexpected life is here. Now the flashes of color were the approaching headlights of autos traveling in file, and the burst of neon and the shape of buildings dark against the night sky, all of it promising curtain up! Kickoff!

Andrew and a couple of friends were in the apartment when we arrived. They had the car unloaded and the baggage in the house in moments. Betty and I had traveled 1,851 miles on our trip back from the island but, in this first summer of my retirement, we have traveled a greater distance than that, beyond sickness and death, past the imagined obstacles of idle time into an understanding that however much time we have left together, Betty and I, it will not be time enough.

Monday Night Football
Tuesday, October 8

I could not teach my sons carpentry because I cannot hammer a nail straight, or work on a motor with them, because I do not understand motors.

I did work with Andrew building models. He was nine or ten. We started with something simple—a cartoon frog. Our second project was a military helicopter. After a time it was clear that Andrew could read blueprints better than I could, and from then on he worked alone.

I was, obviously, not much of an American dad. I couldn't even take the family for a spin in the car because I don't drive, we didn't have a car, and even if I drove and we had a car,

I regard the family spin as an unnatural act. I speak only of *my* family.

What the boys and I could share, a really big thing we could share, was football—watching football, tossing a football around, talking football. Football is a valuable thing, a loved thing. I try, not always successfully, not to scorn other bizarre American rituals because I participate in football worship. My football memory is like my Shakespeare memory; I cannot remember a time in my life without either. I remember taking my football to bed with me when I was a boy, the satisfactory smell of leather, grass, and mud.

Andrew, Mike, and I watched hours of football together, all through their elementary and high school years. Watching football on television is probably when we did more talking with each other than at any other time. Experts on families may find something wrong with that, but a game lasts three hours, after all, and we were relaxed. I don't see how we would have been better off if we had talked while we fished or went on a family spin.

We tossed the ball around on a patch of Central Park we called "Mosedale Field," which is also where the boys played football with their friends, without any supervision from me. We used Mosedale Field until the boys' arms grew so much stronger than mine that they had to come in for my passes, and I was getting out of the way of theirs.

We watched college football, with particular interest in a Nebraska championship squad because a friend of Michael's had a cousin on that team. We were Giants fans, but above all we were Vikings fans. The boys learned disappointment early. When they were very young, my smooth dissembling helped. If the Vikings' best running back didn't gain much yardage, I explained that was because he was "Hard Yard Dave," meaning the yards were particularly fiercely defended when he got the ball. If the Vikes were being truly bloodied, I might suggest a catch, or some other distraction.

Where were Betty and the girls while this was going on? A more skillful father might have induced the girls into joining the fun, but neither Amy nor Laura showed the slightest interest. Betty hated football. She grew to accept it but no more. I mean, I took her to a Super Bowl and she sat on the fifty-yard line, and I am sure she does not remember who played that day.

But most of all the football the boys and I watched was Monday night football. They sometimes were doing other things on the weekend, but Monday was a school day and a workday; and the game came as a relief and a treat. We started watching when Mike was so young he would fall asleep in the first half, face down on the bed. Once when he was sleeping like that, the Vikings did something sudden and positive, and Andrew and I let out howls. Mike raised his head, eyes still closed, applauded, cheered, and fell back to sleep.

Over the course of a dozen years, we must have missed watching some Monday night football games, but I cannot imagine the circumstance. Memory, tradition, and the sense of family connection may explain why I didn't feel I was officially back in New York until last night when I saw ABC's graphic swoop and dive, heard Hank Williams, Jr., jump-start the evening, saw the familiar shot from the blimp, watched the painted and berserk fans, listened to good old Frank and Al and Dan Dierdorf.

Betty and I had been in New York exactly one week. I have been back to CBS. I stopped at the newsroom to see former colleagues and to have Dan Rather sign his new book, which I bought Betty for her birthday.

I bought Betty a couple of other gifts, including Kiri sings Verdi and Puccini to replace our eaten tape. The new packaging of the tape carried a sticker which promises, "Includes 'O Mio Babbino Caro,' featured in the nationally televised commercial for Tott's Champagne." I am in favor of any commercial that wins people to Puccini.

We celebrated Betty's birthday at home. Amy, Laura, Andrew, Matt, Miss Molly, and I. Mike called from Los Angeles. On Saturday, Betty and I attended a wedding in Westchester. A five-piece band played raucous contemporary pop and a string of Glenn Miller hits, and Betty and I danced our feet sore.

Betty went to church Sunday and visited a friend. I dealt with the Sunday newspapers and watched "Sunday Morning." Then on this sixth weekend of National Football League games, I got started with sports talk programs at 10:30, watched pregames, two complete games, broke for dinner, and watched a hideous night game which ended around midnight.

And yet I did not truly believe I was back in New York until the Monday night football. The game was lopsided but interesting because underdog Kansas City walloped Buffalo, which appeared baffled to discover the other team can run, as well as pass, the football. I stayed until the end of the game, again around midnight. A year ago, faced with a day at the office, I would have departed at halftime.

The other day I read a review of a memoir by a writer who says she finds more to dislike as she becomes older. This does not seem to be my condition. I root as strongly as ever watching football, for example, but I no longer hate the other team the way I used to. There is still plenty to hate in this world but for reasons more serious than football.

I do not know if this condition is the result of age or retirement or even if it is permanent. It may take me the rest of the season to find out.

❖ ❖ ❖ ❖ ❖

My self-evaluation of the new, equable me is deflated.

Our television set went on the blink today, Tuesday, and I went into my Rumpelstiltskin routine. I was childish with fury. A pleasant woman at the cable company said she would "send a signal" to our box but this necromancy did no good. They will try to get a repairman here tomorrow. *Dománi. Mañana. Demain. Never.*

I called a neighbor. His set was out, too. I found this comforting. The American League playoffs begin tonight on CBS, the channel most seriously affected, nothing but snow and sibilance. But what I am most upset about is that I will miss "The CBS Evening News." I am possessed by "The CBS Evening News." I have watched it for decades. Watching other networks' news programs is like reading a newspaper in an unfamiliar language. Even during the years I worked in sports, friends knew not to call me when Walter Cronkite was explaining things.

Why did I carry on like the Terrible-Tempered Mr. Bang, the comic page character my sisters said I resembled when I threw a tantrum as a child? I would put this small inconvenience into perspective on the island, if I watched television on the island. Why is this so much more important on the city island than it would be on the country island?

At 6:30, the hour of Dan in New York, I turned to ABC. It is a respectable broadcast, but it is not "The CBS Evening News." I was working in sports when Harry left CBS for ABC in 1972. Betty and I tried watching his evening news broadcast, which was opposite Walter Cronkite.

The experiment didn't last a week. We missed Walter telling us what happened, and we asked ourselves, watching ABC, who are these people reporting from the White House, from Capitol Hill, from Chicago and Dallas? They were not the faces and voices we were accustomed to. How could we trust them?

No one seems to have a beat on television news anymore. I grew up spoiled by radio, listening to Murrow and Sevareid and Shirer and Collingwood at their posts. Now the CBS correspondent in Paris and Rome and Berlin is our correspondent in London, and the bureau that covers South Dakota is located on West Fifty-seventh Street in New York.

I missed seeing Dan, missed hearing the words written by people I know, missed the CBS correspondents. When I checked a little later, the picture was back. I watched some of the ball game, but it wasn't so important now. On the island, I would have understood that from the start.

October Weather

Thursday, October 10

Laura and Molly dropped by our apartment this morning. Laura had an appointment. She, Matt, and Molly are flying to Miami this weekend for the wedding of Laura's college roommate. I think that will be Molly's first trip to Miami, although she is a well-traveled infant.

Betty and I played with the baby until she fell asleep. She slept until Laura returned. After lunch, I walked Laura and Molly to their home, pushing the baby in her stroller, one of the grand perks of grandparenthood. Laura and I chatted while Molly snoozed in her chariot. Babies have an innate sense of royalty; whatever is coming to them, they seem to believe, is no more than their due—gifts, all the attention, being carried and cosseted and transported, no more than their due. Molly lolled as imperiously as a queen.

It was close to a perfect day with a breeze and sunshine and a temperature in the sixties. Why would anyone want to be any place but New York on a day like this? We walked about twenty blocks, passing agreeable New Yorkers, past the El Dorado, the Museum of Natural History, the Dakota, and other monuments that only *seem* as venerable as the pines of Minnesota.

After I saw the ladies home, I returned to our apartment by way of Amsterdam Avenue, listening to Carly Simon sing her sweet sad songs. They are as touching in the racket of city streets as they are in the wind's kiss of the island.

My happiness at that moment was, I realized, a gift of retirement. I would not have had the visit with Laura and Molly, would not have been outdoors in the sun if I were still informing America. Weekdays are the times for mothers and babies and gentlemen in retirement.

Judge Thomas and Professor Hill
Sunday, October 13

Newsday estimated today that about "thirty million homes" viewed live coverage of Friday's hearings on sexual harassment charges against Clarence Thomas, President Bush's nominee for the Supreme Court.

The newspaper said the figure represented about half of all the homes with television sets turned on. I can't imagine what people in the other half looked at.

Betty, Andrew, and I watched from the start of the hearing at ten o'clock in the morning until it shut down for the night. Betty and I took time out for a late afternoon walk, but it was the longest stretch of television viewing I've indulged in that didn't involve football.

If we had not come home from the island, we would not have been so attentive. We didn't pay a lot of attention this summer to Judge Thomas's confirmation hearings. We listened to some news summaries, and I was surprised to hear that never as law student, judge, or private citizen had Clarence Thomas discussed *Roe v. Wade*. I learned from cartoons that he cited as an example of his humble youth that he had had to use an outhouse.

Commentators and participants called Friday's hearings painful, even disgusting. I found the whole show hypnotic and instructive. This was the real thing, not packaged by advertising wizards, this was how things work in our nation's deliberative bodies. We saw some of our best-known legislators, puffed up by themselves and their agents, now celebrated as witty, erudite, and dedicated.

We saw what they were really like. And they vowed that nothing like this must ever happen again.

Judge Thomas may turn out to be Benjamin Cardozo, but there is no doubt that his appointment was political, a stick-it-in-your-ear choice, the kind of politics by ploy much in favor. It guaranteed a political response. That is a nonpartisan observation.

The clash between Judge Thomas and Professor Hill seems to have captivated everyone Betty and I talked with this weekend.

On Saturday we attended a sizeable party honoring friends who recently were married, and on Sunday we attended a sizeable wedding in Westchester. Once the congratulations were out of the way, at both parties, talk turned to the Thomas-Hill hearings.

My sampling at these gatherings showed almost unanimous support for Professor Hill's version of the truth. I see that the national polls lean toward Judge Thomas.

I am not surprised by the contradictions in these findings. Our three younger children attended a small school, grades one through six, run by the Presbyterian Church. They were convinced, on the basis of classroom polls, that McGovern would crush Nixon. We are out of step on the West Side.

Still, I was confounded by some of the senatorial behavior we saw on Friday, especially Senator Hatch's shock over the language Professor Hill said Judge Thomas addressed to her. Senator Hatch could not imagine talk like that from anyone other than "a pervert" or "a psychopathic sex fiend."

I have often wondered where United States senators come from, and it is clearly not from the streets, playgrounds, factories, or offices of our land. I don't mean just here in the wicked East. I have been to Salt Lake City.

Some commentators went along with the politicians and suggested that hearings of this kind debased the Senate. It is difficult to see how this is possible as a general proposition. It seems to me that Senate committees held hearings about what men and women thought and wrote that were far more obscene and dangerous for the nation than anything we were likely to hear from Judge Thomas or Professor Hill. Looking around the world today, who would believe that this society once was paralyzed with fear over an idea so obviously doomed as communism?

People asked me the other day if I didn't miss being in the newsroom during these interesting times. People seem to have trouble understanding that it was wonderful for me to have worked for CBS for thirty years, and now it is wonderful for me *not* to be working there. I explained that if I had been in the newsroom I would not have been able to watch the hearings. I would have been writing some other story, the economy or the latest trend in murders.

I would have missed that lovely, symbolic moment when Senator Simpson, in sympathy with the Thomas cause, quoted, " 'Who steals my purse steals trash.' " "No! Stop!" cried the decent patriot in me. "Go! Go!" cried the evil spectator. The senator, identified as are so many as a lover of Shakespeare, pressed on, " 'But he that filches from me my good name / Robs me of that which not enriches him / And makes me poor indeed.' "

Surely even the Congress of the United States can have

offered few richer, more horrifying moments than a Senator Smiles advancing his cause by quoting to a black man an evil misogynist who is twisting a knife in the soul of the wretched Moor. Then they both go after Desdemona. No commentator pointed this out, although the incident was subjected to much scorn and laughter at the parties we attended this weekend.

Judge Thomas, of course, will be confirmed. The men's club is gathered around him. My comments on this matter center on conservative Republicans. The Democrats in the hearing did approximately nothing. They sat around like dummies.

Echoes

Sunday, October 20

Betty and I have just returned from Maryland, where we spent the weekend in order to visit Betty's mother.

While Betty was at the nursing home Saturday, I took the Metro into Washington. I debarked at Union Station.

When I teach my economics class on the decline of American capitalism in the twentieth century, I will take my students by train from New York to Washington. As we leave the Stalinesque squalor of Penn Station, I will say, "A great building was razed to make room for this plastic and neon nightmare, enriching a few." When we arrive at Union Station, I will say, "American capital once built enduring monuments for profit and to serve the public."

With the collapse of passenger trains in this country, Union Station fell into decay. Congress, thinking hard, decided to turn it into some kind of a visitor's center. It became a warren of plywood and leaks. Then it was restored. Its dark wood gleams, its ceilings vault, its brass shines. With its restaurants and shops, the station always seems busy with people seeking pleasure.

In a way the station symbolizes my version of Washington: a magnificent setting for an inferior cast. Bullet trains with sleepers and dining coaches that feature silver service should sweep into the station from all points. Instead, we have Amtrak.

I walked along Massachusetts Avenue to First Street and up First to East Capitol. I pass buildings I learned about as a schoolboy, the Capitol, the Supreme Court. The Washington I see makes me feel as I did when I sang "My Country 'Tis of Thee." The Washington I don't see fills me with shame, the most murderous national capital in the industrial world.

Strolling with history, I hear a mocking, joyous echo, "Martin, Barton, and Fish," only now it is "Simpson, Specter and Hatch." I shake my head and Echo disappears.

The Folger Shakespeare Library is a monument of the older capitalism. It was brought into being by Henry Clay Folger, a capitalist who spent much of his life accumulating Shakespeariana and the means to house it. The library building was constructed, like the Empire State Building, during the depression by believers in the future.

The library runs the length of a city block. On its walls are bas-reliefs depicting scenes from Shakespeare's plays, Bottom as ass, Romeo as lover, Falstaff as king, and so forth. Inside is one of the world's great research libraries, with more copies of the First Folio than any other institution. I cannot use the research library; I am not a scholar.

I have come to the Folger today just to hang out. I wander in the Great Hall. I linger in the gift shop. I look at the poster for the current production at the theater, *Coriolanus,* one of my thirty-seven favorite plays by Shakespeare. I am irritated by my decision to cancel our subscription to the Folger. I would love to be seeing *Coriolanus* tonight and there is almost always an added resonance to Shakespeare in our nation's capital.

At breakfast this morning, the *Washington Post* told me that a New Age minister and his followers are encamped outside colonial Williamsburg. They want to dig up a churchyard where they believe they will find Francis Bacon's blueprint for a new world order. The New Agers say they will find papers proving that Bacon was Elizabeth's son and that he wrote Shakespeare's plays.

I am enormously reassured. I had thought poor Bacon-as-Shakespeare was buried beyond reach. It now appears he only needs to be dug up.

The New Agers also believe they will find the "original" Constitution of the United States, invalidating the need for the Federal Reserve, the Internal Revenue Service, and the American Medical Association. I would encourage them to dig away. It is time we learned who wrote Shakespeare.

The Joy of Old
Monday, October 28

The "About Men" column in yesterday's *Times* was given over to a piece called "The Joy of Old" by Charles Rembar, an author and lawyer.

He immediately cites one benefit of Old: "Half fares on buses and trains." This kind of bargain, he notes, is savored most by those who lived through the depression.

I agree with that, but as the article continues it demonstrates that one umbrella will not cover all of the Old. Rembar writes, "It is hard . . . to find time for recreation. In Old— unless you are retired, a mistake if you like your work—

people tend to demand your presence."

The law office may have more need of the Old than the newsroom does, but in any case retirement for me is the best part of being old, loitering around the premises with Betty, just as I figured it would be months ago.

I loved my work, and I miss my colleagues, but I wake up singing because I do not have to go to an office. I walk out for the newspapers. I sit at this desk each morning and write. But I do not have to go to the office.

Betty and I may not see each other for hours. But I know that she is near. I hear her voice. We always eat lunch together. "For better or worse but not for lunch" is an old joke that so far does not apply to us.

"You're not really retired," friends say because they know I am writing. But I know I am a retired fellow with a project.

Minnesota played Atlanta last night in the seventh game of the World Series, which is a definition of the Big Game. The Giants also played the Redskins last night, which was even bigger around here, since New Yorkers and Washingtonians are as provincial as any people anywhere.

I switched back and forth between the games. I didn't worry about how late the game might run. I wore my Braves cap and waved my Twins homer hankie, and I turned to the football game between innings.

I worked thirty years in television, and I never learned the location of the bunker where commercials are coordinated between sports events, so that innings end just as time outs are called. Commercials collusion is the only conspiracy I believe in.

I didn't get to bed until after 1:00 A.M. From now on, the time I go to sleep is of no importance. I can, if I feel like it, obey the advice of the father in a Max Shulman novel: "Sleep till noon and screw them all."

Joseph Papp
Friday, November 1

On this date in 1604, *Othello* was presented on stage for the first time. On this date in 1611, London saw the first production of *The Tempest*. So I heard early this morning on WQXR-FM. How pleasant, I thought, to awaken to these Shakespeare notes.

Then I remembered. Joseph Papp died yesterday.

I hustled out of bed and down to Broadway. I bought a copy of every New York newspaper and returned to the apartment to read the obituaries and appraisals at breakfast.

Papp was by general agreement the most influential American theater figure of his time. I cannot think of an impresario, *ever,* who had more influence. He produced more than 350 plays. Three of them won Pulitzer prizes. His productions also won 92 Obie, 28 Tony, and 17 Drama Desk awards. He produced *Hair,* the prototype rock musical. He produced *A Chorus Line,* which ran longer than any other show in Broadway history and grossed almost fifty million dollars, most of which Papp put back in his theater.

Joe Papp did all this by way of William Shakespeare. I don't know another story like it. I knew Papp somewhat. I interviewed him once as a newspaperman and a couple of other times when I was writing for television.

(His ex-wife, a therapist, turned up as an observer at a psychodrama class I attended as part of my counseling when I quit drinking. Psychodrama was not for me, although I was game to try anything. What I remember from that class was talking with an art professor who said he had no problem with alchohol and was present only at his daughter's urging. His face was the color of boiled ham.)

Betty and I are charter subscribers to Papp's Shakespeare Marathon, which aims to produce "all thirty-six" of Shakespeare's plays. A couple of years ago, we left our tickets at home. We knew our names were in a festival computer, and we were explaining this to an usher when Papp wandered by and identified us by name, calling us "great supporters of the festival." Papp obviously was a man who had memorized many names and who, in my case, did not hold a grudge.

Because the last time I had seen him before that encounter was at a preview of a ghastly production of *Measure for Measure* he himself directed in the park. It was so bad I could not believe my eyes, or my ears. Papp was in the audience, and at the intermission, I reintroduced myself to him and asked, "Are you doing this on purpose?" He was understandably irritated. We had a brief, heated discussion, something more than the State Department's frank exchange of views. He said *Measure for Measure* was a romantic comedy like *As You Like It.* Perhaps he believed that.

I heard many stories about Joe Papp's arrogance. I don't doubt them. He was a mover and shaker and, without excusing bad behavior, it is true that movers and shakers make many decisions, not all of them wise, including decisions on how to handle people.

What I know is that Joe Papp is the one person who had the idea of putting on Shakespeare, free, and so far as one person can do anything by himself, did it by himself. He was a slum kid who discovered Shakespeare in the public library.

Papp was all New York. I cannot imagine him coming from any other place on the planet, an old lefty who knew how to get money from the powerful to encourage plays full of protest and subversive energy. In the last year of his life, he turned down federal money the festival badly needed because the money came attached to a ridiculous provision about obscenity.

Through the 1960s and 1970s and 1980s and including a date last summer, Betty and I sat on certain warm nights before the stage in the park. A murmur of crowd and auto traffic whispered down Central Park West. The obligatory plane throbbed overhead. Then the lights would dim and the words of an Englishman dead these many centuries would come alive. The traffic hum disappeared, the audience quieted, and for a time, just for a time, we learned by means of magic some things that life is about.

I don't mean to be romantic. Casts were often indifferent. The weather wasn't always ideal. Once we sat in a downpour that cut short a performance of *Much Ado* because of the threat of lightning. The audience protested the cancellation. People sat, drenched, with soggy newspapers over their heads, begging for the show to continue. In an age of *The Terminator,* we came off the streets and begged for Shakespeare in the rain.

Linda Weiner used the word *privilege* in her column about Papp today. It is the right word. We were privileged to share this city and this theater with him. Joe Papp never forgot. He said, "If I had had to pay, it is doubtful I would have read the plays of Shakespeare."

Inside New York

As I wandered through the living room this afternoon, the sunshine suddenly brightened, and I looked out the window into a shower of yellow leaves. I had never seen this before. We live on the sixth floor, higher than any tree on our block.

Yellow leaves rose like a geyser and then showered down, fluttering and graceful, a lovely trick of the wind as it pushed through the valley of our street and picked up fallen leaves.

I owe the vision to my retirement. I would not have seen anything like that in the CBS newsroom. I see New York differently, now that I am retired.

People who aren't from New York sometimes ask me why

we live here. I am not as irritated by this as I should be. If I asked a man from anyplace else in this country why he chooses to live there, I would properly be regarded as a boor. But it seems to be part of being an American to ask a New Yorker why he lives in the continent's greatest city.

My daily rounds are like something out of a Frank Capra movie. Neighbors in our building, people from other buildings on the street, the fellows at the newsstand, the young man who has just taken over the drugstore where we have shopped for thirty-five years, clerks at the two neighborhood groceries we shop at, the security guard next door, all are as familiar to me as sirens in the night. (The siren, police, or fire, or ambulance, means that someone is trying to help someone.)

New York, like Shakespeare's London and Villon's Paris, is dangerous, crass and rude, but the New Yorkers I encounter daily are as pleasant as people I've known anywhere. It shouldn't be necessary to say this. It didn't used to be, but it is now.

No one catches a city's problems, or a city's character, as well as someone who lives there. I think you have to experience a lifetime of Minneapolis–St. Paul winters to joke about them as ruefully as Twin Cities residents do, and I think strange California is best understood by Californians.

The other night, Betty and I heard *L'Elisir d'Amore* at the Met. We walked out of there agreeing we probably would never hear that opera sung any better. On the bus ride home, two women discussed the opera. A woman across the way asked them what they were so enthusiastic about. They explained. A rather shabby looking man wearing a baseball cap said to the air, "Ah, Donizetti!"

The news seems more real in the city than it does in the country. Magic Johnson's recent announcement that he had the AIDS virus and was retiring from basketball hit me more profoundly than did the collapse of the Soviet Union, which was filtered through islandness.

Most of the trees on our block now stand in pretty

flower beds, thanks to our new block association. It is a visible improvement which lifts the spirit and is the work of a few people. I am not one of them, but Betty and Andrew were.

If I were still writing news, I would have been as ignorant of the source of this neighborliness as any tourist.

I Hate Television

Sunday, November 16

No wonder people hate television.

I am told by Betty that a company is taping something down the street for an NBC series called "Law and Order," which I bet is about anything but. I saw no sign of activity, although the television people have effectively closed off our street to parking since Thursday.

On that afternoon, a row of orange pylons suddenly appeared across the street, stretching almost the length of the block, like insolent little creatures from outer space. A workman told Betty there would be filming Friday night and, meanwhile, she could park the car on our side of the street.

Parked cars must be moved at stated intervals from one side of the street to another in New York, to make garbage pickup easier. (There are few back alleys in New York.) Thanks to budget cutbacks, garbage now is collected less often and so alternate side of the street parking, as it is called, is less troublesome than it used to be. (The budget crisis also eased life for dog owners, since there are fewer pet police to ticket unleashed criminals.)

The orange outer space aliens apparently bred during the night because by Friday they lined both sides of the street and Central Park West in both directions. There was no place for us to park. Now, we were told, shooting would take place today, Monday. I said nothing to the security people who passed along the news. They were hired to do this. It was not their decision.

This was a damned nuisance and made me hate television. Our parking space was taken from us for a series I never heard of, no offense intended for I have never heard of most series. The gall of the thing angered me. By what right did these people barge in and disrupt life in a quiet neighborhood with no advance warning? What way is this to run a city?

A notice appeared in our lobby Saturday, more than a day after our space was swiped, but it could have been a joke for all I knew. The notice said the street was closed so a production company could film an episode of "Law and Order."

Betty and I wasted a lot of time this weekend, driving around the neighborhood, looking for a place to park within a few blocks of our apartment. The streets were jammed with others in the herd, grazing for parking space. Although she did the driving, Betty took this in better humor than I did.

Retirement may be spoiling me. I resent any interruption of my good time.

Betty and I snuck off for an afternoon movie. Seeing a movie on a weekday brings an extra reward, like playing hooky. We saw the just-released *Beauty and the Beast,* which added to the illusion that we were somehow cutting class. I hadn't seen a full-length cartoon in decades. I worried when

I first saw Belle, who seemed to be wearing Snow White's old outfit, but I soon lost myself in the movie.

There were younger class-cutters than we attending the matinee. A small voice at the end of our row said, "Oh, oh," during a tense moment, and at one desperate turn an older voice muttered, "Oh, shit!" Behind us, a boy said as Belle appeared in a formal gown, "That's the girl I'm gonna marry when I grow up."

I wished Molly were old enough to see *Beauty and the Beast*. By the time she sees it, it will likely be on a television screen. She should see it in a big dark theater, in the company of strangers.

I watched a lot of football this weekend and loved television again. College football Saturday, three pro games on Sunday. I worked for a great medium. No wonder the average American watches seven hours of television a day and by middle age has spent eleven years in front of the set.

Still, I am sore about this "Law and Order" outfit sealing off our block. No one from the company took the time to find out if there was a block association that could use a small donation. Is that too much to ask?

The city, as far as I could tell, did nothing. These people, the "Law and Order" people, I mean, must have to get some kind of permit from the city. What's happened to this city, anyway?

A couple of summers ago, while we were away on the island, the people who ran the corner grocery locked up one night and walked away. Like that. I guess they turned off the electricity, because in the summer heat the grocery soon began to stink. People living in the apartment above the store reportedly called the police, the health department, emergency numbers. Nothing happened.

By the time we returned to the city, weeks later, the stench stretched across the sidewalk—rotting meat, butter, eggs, milk souring in the city summer. Months later, workers in gas masks with decontamination equipment entered the store. As of today it may be cleaned up, but it remains unoccupied.

I returned Betty's Italian novels to the St. Agnes library

today. I listened to my *Twelfth Night* tape, Paul Scofield and Siobhan McKenna. The sound faded while I was in the library. I inserted new batteries. Not a wheel turned. The tape player didn't work. I walked home mourning my dead Aiwa, figuring to replace it as soon as I could. As I walked in the front door I had a hunch. I checked. I had put in one of the batteries backwards.

My computer was cold this morning. I discovered, after much fuming, that I had forgotten to plug it in. I can't remember why I unplugged it in the first place. My mistakes seem to get more stupid. I tell myself it has nothing to do with age. I am doing more advanced things.

Thanksgiving

Friday, November 28

Yesterday, for the first time in seven years, I shared Thanksgiving with my family.

It is possible to take the holiday off at CBS News, but it meant that other writers with younger children would work, so I sacrificed myself. This enhanced the feeling of martyrdom that comes from working on holidays, one of journalism's richer rewards.

We went to Betty's sister's house in Connecticut, as the family has almost every Thanksgiving since Betty and I have been married. It was the one time of the year when the families were sure to assemble. We see our children and Barbara's children grow up in family photographs taken at Thanksgiving.

Our numbers were diminished this year. Russ is dead and Helen went into the nursing home not long after last Thanksgiving. Barbara's youngest son is in Sweden, and Andy and Mike are on the West Coast. We started the day with toasts to the absent.

The legendary, traditional Thanksgiving feast followed, the kind that leaves you grateful and unable, without abstaining for an hour or two, to have your way with three kinds of pie and coffee.

Small children, in the shape of Barbara's grandsons, were present. Small children are essential for a family Thanksgiving. Molly and her parents stopped in before proceeding to join Matt's family for dinner.

Thanksgiving afternoon is time for football watching. It always has been. I used to watch the big college games on radio when I was a boy. College football was much bigger than the professional game. My uncle and I were the only males at our Thanksgiving table—he had four daughters— and I could never understand why he wanted to sit and visit with those women when he could come to the radio with me and see the Penn-Cornell game.

I think Thanksgiving is the toughest of holidays to spend alone. It is so purely a family time. I remember my first Thanksgiving away from home. I was in the navy in San Diego and we ate turkey in eighty-degree weather and there was tinsel on the palm trees. Bing Crosby sang "White Christmas" everywhere I turned.

New York showed me how to spend a bachelor Thanksgiving. Two Manhattan cocktails, followed by a restaurant meal, followed by a theater matinee. I saw Geraldine Page in *The Rainmaker* and Julie Harris in *The Lark* my first two Thanksgivings in New York.

Then I met Betty and Thanksgiving became a family time again. At this feast there seems to be an almost physical presence of the dead and others absent who shared the joys of earlier Thanksgivings. This is not a gloomy, but a reassuring thought for me because the family endures. It changes but it endures; the family confirms the argument of the ancients: everything changes, nothing dies.

Pearl Harbor

Saturday, December 7

I'm not sure where I was when I heard that the Japanese had attacked Pearl Harbor. If you were alive at the time, you are supposed to recall the moment. I was more or less alive, being a fifteen-year-old male.

My recollection is that I was in bed when Mother rushed into the room, announcing, "The Japanese have bombed Pearl Harbor!"—as if she, as if I, had the vaguest notion where Pearl Harbor is. She turned on my desk radio, raised the window shade, flooding the room with Milwaukee daylight, and departed. I don't recall being particularly shocked. War had been approaching for so long, striding down the street toward us, that it was as if we greeted a tardy guest, "Well, here you are at last!"

It seems to me that I was in assembly, struggling with "The Lay of the Last Minstrel," when over the school public address system I heard President Roosevelt ask Congress for a declaration of war. Even a high school student knew that speech was historic.

My favorite uncle assured my mother that the war would be over in six months, "the Japs" melting before the onslaught of American boys. He had been in the trenches in World War I, so I figured he knew. War, of course, stirs up ignorant hate, and my friends and I slipped into easy racism. The enemy was the Jap, bucktoothed, slant-eyed, yellow-bellied. At the movies we sang along to "To Be Specific, It's Our Pacific" and "We Have Got to Slap the Dirty Little Jap."

Hate turned more to the Japanese than to the European enemies. I do not recall any outcry when Americans of Japanese descent were herded off to camps, although Mother said that if the government were consistent, it would put barbed wire around Milwaukee, where many people had German blood.

The war was not over in six months. Within a short time, one of my brothers-in-law was on a PBY in the Pacific, the other was in the army in India.

None of my friends or I gave thought to life after high school beyond going into the service. In our confidence and ignorance, this was relaxing. Choice, which is hard, had been removed from our lives. The idea of *not* serving in the armed forces was disgraceful. I doubt that's been true of any war we have fought since. One effect of war is aphrodisiacal. Love did seem imperilled, kisses stolen. I think of courage and death when I think of World War II, but I also think of girls.

Immediately on my graduation in 1944, along with just about all of my friends, I went into the service. None of the people close to me in Milwaukee died in the war, although some of the upper classmen were killed. And my island leader . . .

The book fell from a shelf this summer as I was looking

for something else. It was published by Carleton College. The epigraph is from Laurence Binyon: "They shall not grow old, as we that are left grow old: / Age shall not weary them, nor the years condemn. / At the going down of the sun and in the morning / We shall remember them."

The book says 1,502 men and women from this small college served in the war. Fifty-four of them died. From this single small college. Do you multiply that for every college and factor in the big state universities, remembering that the great majority of people serving in World War II had never been to college?

I looked at the faces of these men who died young. Each has a page. The faces are bright and full of anticipation. What they share is that none got a chance at the best part of life, which is being an independent adult.

Here my island leader is. He was "killed by the explosion of a land mine on March 19, 1945, while driving his truck to a forward position during an attack on the Siegfried line." He had been a radio operator and an interpreter. In less than two months, the war in Europe was over.

He looks out from the page more solemnly than I remember him from island summers. He was just enough wiser and just enough older to be the natural leader of our small group, the inventor of running games, the one who lighted the biggest firecracker.

He loved fishing so much he even got me to go fishing with him. He and I portaged in to a nearby lake one summer night and at sundown we caught bass as quickly as we could haul them into the boat. We threw the fish back, for the sport of it. This is my only fishing story.

He was just enough older to be our leader, just enough older to be called up early in the war. The important statistic in any war is one. The one who didn't come back.

There is ample injustice in the world, and I do not have to rummage around in the past to find it, but I think of my sterling friend and what a fine man he would have been, and I think we have let him down, and all the others who died in the war.

Fetes

Our holiday season includes two birthdays and our wedding anniversary. Retirement gave me more time to celebrate.

Monday, December 16

I am sixty-six years old today. Sixty-six is an age I never thought I would achieve because it is an ancient age to a child, even to a young man, although millions of us who reach sixty-six realize how short the trip has been.

I am grateful for each birthday. I am sorry for people who don't enjoy their birthdays. Making it in good health through another year is a cause for celebration.

For reasons of scheduling, Mosedale's Birthday (Observed) was celebrated yesterday. Betty and I went to church, then I took the bus to the Metropolitan Opera and stood in line to buy myself a ticket to see *Turandot,* since I will be out of the country when our subscription performance is sung. I did some Christmas shopping.

Betty spent the day in the kitchen, working as hard as she ever did for one of the children's birthdays. The menu, of my choice, was Basic American Male Before Health Considerations: filet mignon, mashed potatoes, green beans, tomato and onion salad, and white cake with butterscotch frosting and ice cream. Except for Mike, who was in Los Angeles, all the children attended, along with Matt and Molly.

Laura said she heard that the doctors up at Harvard have just announced that sixty-six is the prime of life for the American male. I used to make this birthday announcement myself. "Children," I would say, "I heard the greatest news at work today. The doctors up at Harvard have just discovered that [thirty-eight, forty-seven, fifty-six] is the absolute prime for a man in this country, the age at which he is at the top of his game, mentally and physically." The children rolled their eyes. Now they go along with the gag.

On the other hand, I am always reading or hearing news items about "elderly" men or women who, it turns out, are sixty-one or sixty-three years old.

I feel much better at sixty-six than I did at, say, forty. This is one of the great benefits of not drinking alcohol if you cannot drink.

I opened my presents after dinner, in front of the Christmas tree. Betty and the children bought me every book or tape that I hoped for.

As I walked along Central Park South the other evening, I noticed guests leaving their hotels, climbing into taxis headed for the airports. I suddenly thought how painful it would be for me if I had to leave the city at that moment, the darkness just beginning to fill up Central Park, the lights beckoning in the sinful, joyous towers. I thought I would hate to leave this city.

My family, books, shows, and the city. Why wouldn't I welcome birthdays, to be reminded of these?

❖ ❖ ❖ ❖ ❖

Anniversary
Monday, December 23

Betty is sleeping like a bride this predawn after our thirty-fifth wedding anniversary, as I write this at the desk of room 814 in our motel. We drove to Maryland yesterday so that Betty can spend some Christmas time with her mother in the nursing home.

The motel offered us a room with twin beds. Betty got on the phone and in a Shakespearean minute, we were in a different room, with a bed the size of Bosworth Field.

My thirty-fifth anniversary gift to Betty cost whatever a blank audio tape costs. It is a selection of some of our favorite songs, lifted off records we own. We haven't heard some of the records in years. The songs are mostly highly sentimental. We've been lucky in the music of our days. We met and married, for example, in 1956, when *My Fair Lady* and *The Most Happy Fella* opened. Our tape begins with "Mack the Knife" from *The Threepenny Opera*, which we saw on one of our first dates.

We listened to these songs of our life together as soon as we checked into the motel. Then we visited Betty's mother and ate a fine roast beef dinner nearby. Now I am watching Betty sleep and feeling sentimental.

Since *Gone with the Wind* is one of our great national myths, Anna Quindlen uses the novel to identify men as Ashley (husband) and Rhett (boyfriend). I do not mean to betray my sex, but I believe that most American men *think* of themselves as Rhett but are really Ashley. In his heart, the male is master of the situation, ready to face down opinion, a great lover, a wit. In reality, he is Ashley, well-intended, decent when he can afford to be, but just a beat behind the band.

I think most men work hard at what they do in part to hide the suspicion that whatever they do, what their wives do is more important. A man cannot bear a child. This is by no means a woman's only function, but it is the function which immediately sets her apart from the male, whose only role in the process can literally be put in cold storage these days.

Gerontologists have noticed that elderly men tend to fall apart, or even die, shortly after their wives die. Widows live practically forever. The ways in which women are superior to men are so obvious and so many that you would think even a man might recognize them.

I may be victim of this sentimental occasion, but I wonder at all the things Betty had managed to do. Betty is special to me, but millions of other women are wives and mothers who manage a household and hold a job and never, ever, think of themselves as "Supermom." It is just like a man to call a fellow Superman simply because he can jump over a building.

❖ ❖ ❖ ❖ ❖

Michael's Birthday

Tuesday, December 24

Michael was born on this day, the morning of Christmas Eve in 1963.

Betty and I spoke to him on the phone from Room 814 this morning. He is writing free-lance newspaper pieces in Los Angeles, farther away from us than he has ever been.

The night of December 23 in 1963, New York was filling with snow as I came home late from a CBS Sports Christmas party. Betty said it was time to get to the hospital. It would have been impossible to find a taxi in that snow. Nothing was moving. The city was preternaturally quiet. A Quaker couple had recently moved into our building, and the husband offered to take us to the hospital in their car.

I agreed to help him shovel the car out from the snow bank that was piling up around it. But I had received a new red corduroy shirt for my birthday, and I decided I wanted to wear it for the birth of our fourth child. I was sitting wooz-ily on the bed, removing pins from my new shirt, when Betty appeared in the bedroom doorway.

"Johnny," she said. "I really think we had better hurry."

What I heard in her voice got me moving. On the street, we found our friend ready to go. Other cars on the street were covered with snow.

"How did you get shoveled out so quickly?" I asked as we climbed into the car.

He said, "It's the darndest thing. I had just started shov-eling when three men came by, out of the dark. I think they were Hispanics. I said there was a lady upstairs about to have a baby. Could they help?" He shook his head. "They didn't say a word. They disappeared for a moment, then returned with shovels. In a minute I was dug out. Then, they just walked away toward the park before I could offer them money or thank them."

I don't know what would have happened if those good fellows hadn't come by. We got Betty to the hospital just in time. I walked once around the block before the doctor told me we had a new son. It was shortly after midnight.

That made two girls, two boys. Each child in our family had a sister, each had a brother.

At Christmas Eve services tonight, I will think, as I always do, about Michael's birth and the births of his sisters and brother, of beginnings.

Amy was born on an October night. Betty and I had seen Emlyn Williams in his one-man show about Dylan Thomas. When we got home, Betty said quietly, "Johnny, how would you like to have a baby tonight?"

Laura was born on a sunny June day. In the labor room, Betty grimaced. I was about to call for every drug in the phar-macopoeia when she said, "Could you please ask them to turn off that Muzak?"

Andrew was born after Betty and I had waited a time in the hospital, a long enough time for her to tell me we were about to have our first son. I bet her my smoking habit against that. Andrew arrived and, after a hideous time, I quit cigarettes.

I've told our children that the most important days of my life are my wedding day and the days they were born and there is still no contest about that.

✤ ✤ ✤ ✤ ✤

Christmas

There are twelve days of Christmas. When I worked at the evening news, Christmas was half a day.

The children rose early and played with small gifts stuffed in Christmas stockings. After Betty and I were awake, we all ate breakfast. Then, sitting at the foot of the tree, I dispensed presents.

Sometime between ten and eleven in the morning, I left for work, and it was just another day at the office. I deserve no sympathy, however. The father who is present for the opening of the gifts enjoys the best part of the day. Any emotional crashes by the children occur after the male lion is in his workplace.

It is a blessing of retirement that Christmas for Betty and me this year stretched over three days. She spent the early part of Christmas Eve at the nursing home. She sat in the dining room while her mother ate. Many of the people there are in bad shape, yet Betty said they expressed gratitude for being so well looked after this Christmas season.

Betty and I ate in the motel restaurant. It would have been better to share Christmas Eve dinner in our home with our children. It would have been worse a whole lot of other places.

We found a church a few miles away. Services began with a half hour of choir singing. Then we sang "Once in Royal David's City" and "What Child Is This?" and "Joy to the World" and Christina Rossetti's "In the Bleak Midwinter."

The service was haunted by the reassuring ghosts of Christmas eves past, so that in the Maryland church, I was back in the cozy church which was blanketed in Milwaukee snow, back on the hanger deck in the Pacific overarched by more stars than I would ever again see, back in the Hell's Kitchen church, the Fifth Avenue church, the Upper West Side church.

We spent Christmas morning with Helen while she opened her presents. We drove back to New York borne on the current of Christmas song. The girls, including Molly, came to the apartment for our official Christmas day. We opened our gifts. If Molly stayed six months old for the rest of the century, she could not use all the gifts she has already received.

But her best gift was us, the gift of us, loving adults who held her and hugged her and kissed her and laughed at her. She was our best gift, too. A child's presence is the timeless Christmas sermon: love with no conditions.

❖ ❖ ❖ ❖ ❖

New Year

Thursday, January 2, 1992

Whether or not you attend a party, you should be with someone you love on New Year's Eve. Going into our thirty-fifth New Year celebration together, Betty and I shared surprises pleasant and unpleasant.

On Monday, I walked to Coliseum Books on West Fifty-seventh Street to buy myself an engagement calendar, which S. Claus overlooked this Christmas, perhaps figuring that the retired don't have engagements. Coliseum Books is one of the few tangible examples of human progress I have seen in my lifetime. It stands on the site of an auto showroom.

The customer is never disappointed in a well-conducted bookstore. If he does not find what he is looking for, another book will summon him in the manner of the sharper Sheldon Leonard accosting Jack Benny, "Psssst, buddy! Over here!" I found a dandy engagement calendar in a baseball mode, and

I decided to look around a bit before leaving, a kind of book-buyer's tic which always costs money but never much money since books remain the best buy in American commerce.

They gleamed like a mountain of gold. Three small shelves of brightly covered new paperback editions of Trollope. There were the familiar, loved titles. And there—I almost swooned, as a book-buyer will understand—there was *An Old Man's Love,* Trollope's final novel, which Betty and I have been seeking for years and years.

Trollope was only a name to me until a night in 1976 when Heywood Hale Broun, the most widely read man I have ever known, discoursed on Trollope over black bean soup in a restaurant in the countryside of Puerto Rico, where a group of us was gathered for a heavyweight title fight.

Back in New York on June 14—the date is written on the title page—I picked up *Barchester Towers.* This novel asks the question, "Who is to rule the diocese of Barchester?" The degree of your interest in that question is a measure of your susceptibility to Trollope. There are plenty of people who don't like Trollope. They are called brutes.

Our Trollopes are frequently inscribed to Betty from me or to me from Betty. They were our ultimate gift. Even Trollope, or at least available Trollope, was finite, however, and it has been at least five years since we have discovered a new title.

I mean to reread Trollope now that I am retired. Can *Doctor Thorne* possibly be as charming as I remember it being? If I grow infirm, I hope someone will read Trollope aloud to me. Shakespeare might become too difficult, but I am sure that Trollope will warm my old bones.

There *are* people who haven't read Trollope who aren't brutes. I was a bit hasty there. But Trollope readers seem to be a special band and often, when you mention his name in a crowded room, a few people shoot you glances of recognition. It is like being in the French resistance in a room full of Gestapo officers.

I hurried home with *An Old Man's Love.* It is an Oxford University Press World Classic edition, but in paper. Betty won't mind. She was shopping downtown, and Andrew and I were to meet her at Loew's Pentaplex, or whatever the number is up to. I inscribed the book and put it on her pillow. I imagined her eyes when she sees the book.

As Andrew and I stepped out of our apartment, a maid who works for people across the hall pointed to an adjoining apartment. The door was ajar, the door frame splintered. We called out a few times. No answer. We could see from the door that a bedroom had been ransacked. Andrew went to meet his mother before she got to worrying about us. I left a message for the super. I called our police precinct (What far-sighted person put the number in our Rolodex?).

An intelligent-sounding woman answered the phone. I told her what had happened. "Did you go into the apartment?" she asked. "No," I said. "I didn't think it would be a good idea." "You're right," she said. "It wouldn't."

A policeman arrived promptly. Someone located the woman who lived in the burglarized apartment. The thief had been in a hurry. He had stolen some things but he left others. The apartment door probably was forced with a crowbar, the policeman said, or possibly with a kick.

When Betty and Andrew returned from the movies, she spoke with the locksmith who was working on the broken door frame. Our protection is pretty good, but we will have him make it better. A determined thief can get into any dwelling, but we want to make him work for it.

Burglary is hardly big news in New York, or, these days, most other places in this country that I know about. We find burglar alarm systems in the suburban homes of friends. Our apartment has not been broken into but our island cabin has. A thief or thieves entered it during the winter years ago.

The burglary reminded us how vulnerable we are. It also reminded us that our most valued material possessions are worth nothing to a thief—photograph albums of the children and friends, books, music.

Betty and I saw *The Double Life of Veronique* on New Year's Eve. There was a time in my life when I would have thought a movie on New Year's Eve was either a dull idea or only a preliminary, and while we enjoyed this enigmatic film, it was not the highpoint of this New Year's Eve.

We walked home from the theater, up Columbus Avenue. The revelers crowded the street, heading from one party to another. No one we saw was out of control. We stopped in the restaurant to wish Amy a happy new year. Back home we climbed into our night clothes. Betty drank a beer. I drank a Diet Dr Pepper. We found a television channel that showed the traditional New Year's madness in Times Square.

Then we turned off all the lights except those on the Christmas tree. We sat, just the two of us, listening to *L'Elisir d'amore*. I thought of past New Year's Eves, times of too much drinking, times of wonderful parties, even after I quit drinking, times we went to the theater. And I thought, I am sixty-six years old and retired and I do not have to go to an office tomorrow and here I am with Betty and the night before us. I thought I have never had a better New Year's Eve.

Waking Up

Wednesday, January 15

For the past couple of weeks, I have been waking up in the early morning hours, around 3:30 or 5:00 A.M., just as I often did for the last years I had to go to an office. I figure that in my working-at-the-office days some rowdy watchman called, "Job alert!"

When I wake up early, I steal from the bedroom so as not to wake Betty. I take a pillow, and I go to a little room and lie down and listen to the radio. It doesn't make much difference what I listen to. I go back to sleep.

I am waking like this because I know I am going back to an office. In thirteen days I will be flying to Geneva, on my way to write about the winter Olympics. And so this idiot sentry rouses me in the small hours. I awaken to thoughts of packing, making sure my passport and plane tickets are in place, along with my pre-Olympic accreditations. I think of ice hockey, the biathalon, the luge, which have not disturbed my sleep before. I awaken to thoughts of Puccini, doorknobs, toasters, Shakespeare, Bernie Bierman, cold weather, Muhammad Ali, the American political show.

Anxiety thoughts about packing will always be with me. I never sleep well the night before a big trip, sometimes not for several nights. I used to arrive on the island knock-kneed with fatigue. When I fly to Europe I am tired before jet lag strikes.

I am thinking of Puccini because I see *Turandot* a week from Thursday. I am rereading the libretto and listening to our tape of Birgit Nilsson, Tebaldi, and Björling. I will not hear it sung so well.

I am thinking of doorknobs because after the recent break-in across the way, we have had our door reinforced, and that required a new doorknob. Our doorknob now looks like all the other doorknobs in our building; i.e., not as good as the old doorknob. Our old doorknob seemed to be solid brass. It was solid something, and it had an engraved design. Our new doorknob is characterless and appears to be made of spun sugar.

I am thinking of toasters because this country seems no longer able to manufacture a good, reliable toaster. The toaster we got when we were married lasted for years. I think our naughty dog Bounce finally did something to it, or caused something to be done to it. Since then, we have owned a half dozen toasters, and none of them lasted more than a few years. They didn't work well to begin with.

I was with Betty when she bought a top-of-the-line toaster a couple of years ago, and now it doesn't work. We recently have been entertained, even captivated, by the spectacle of the president of the United States leading a bunch of auto tycoons and other manufacturers to Japan, where they complained about unfair trade practices.

237

The reaction Betty and I had was: Do the Japanese make toasters? I think if we bought a Japanese toaster and it quit working after a couple of years, the president of the toaster company would fly across the Pacific and fix the device.

I awake thinking of Shakespeare because I am usually thinking of Shakespeare, and because a friend recently took Betty and me to a screening of Orson Welles's "restored masterpiece" *Othello*. It seemed to me that the problems with the movie are beyond restoration. It is beautifully framed. It is photographed without regard to requirements of the text, so that we noticed the pictures not the play.

I am thinking about Bernie Bierman, who coached University of Minnesota football teams back in the 1930s and '40s because I am reading and hearing a good deal about Minnesota as the site of this year's Super Bowl. So far in the stories I have read about the state's athletic heritage I have encountered no mention of the Bierman teams, which were rated the best in the nation. Their prowess embittered my childhood, growing up in Milwaukee and vacationing on the island, knowing each year that Wisconsin would be a final, November step up the ladder of glory for its rival.

In Bierman's day, in my youth, a player was expected to perform on both offense and defense. This made the game more interesting, I think, and you certainly saw better all-around athletes than you do today. The players today may be bigger, faster, and stronger, but a third-and-long specialist is not as satisfying to watch as a triple threat man or a great runner who is also great against the run.

I think about cold weather because sissy sportswriters from the effete coasts are whining that they may be cold in Minneapolis in January and because seasonably cold weather finally arrived in New York this week. We have had nothing but those warm days and nights when gasses rise from the fens and fell people. Stomach and respiratory flu seem epidemic. The illness I believe comes with warm winter weather.

The other day the television weather man said it was seventeen above zero, clear and windy. Then he cupped his hands and whispered, "With the wind chill, it feels like it is twenty-five below zero." Well, I have been outdoors in twenty-five degrees below zero weather and it does not feel at all like seventeen above. And feels like what to whom? It feels like twenty-five below to me, to my strapping sons, to my aging mother-in-law, to my seven-month-old granddaughter?

It was seventeen degrees above zero, cold and windy. That is all a sensible person needs to know before stepping out. The "wind chill" is only another example of people looking for ways to make other people feel worse.

I think about Muhammed Ali, whose fiftieth birthday is coming up next week. He was the most important sports figure of my lifetime. For a while it was said his was the most famous face in the world.

I was late coming to admire Ali, except as a fighter. I thought the Black Muslims of the time were a hate group and I thought Ali's taunts about whipping Floyd Patterson's "Christian ass" were ugly and dangerous. I let my estimate of the man affect my perception of his skill, always a mistake in judging an artist.

Ali came to mean something for generations younger than mine. Some of what he meant was good. He defied the draft, which cost him a lot of money and four years of his professional life. He questioned the Vietnam war before a lot of intellectuals did. He goaded the establishment. His self-promotion spawned many cheap imitations, but originality always does.

Ali was funny and irreverent, and he was as good at his work as anyone I have ever seen. Well, Sugar Ray Robinson defines boxing for me, and Joe Louis is my hero. But it was a blessing to watch Ali's moves and the snake strike of his fists, and two of his fights with Joe Frazier were models of the craft and reminders of how much more courageous and elemental it can be to fight with fists instead of with guns.

I wake thinking of politics. I will be in France next month when four years ago and eight years ago and twelve years ago I was in New Hampshire for the primary. The president of the United States vomited on the prime minister of Japan last week. The campaign begins. Not even Mencken would have believed the spectacle.

The End of the Beginning

Friday, January 31

It is one year ago today that I walked away from it, leaving the CBS newsroom in New York.

I am writing this late in the afternoon in room 201, next to the elevator, in the Hotel Welcomes in Moutiers, a community of five thousand people in a valley of the French Alps. I am a five-minute walk from the International Broadcast Center, where I will write about the winter Olympic games for CBS Sports.

(The IBC, as it is called, was constructed for the games on the 7½-acre site of a razed steel mill. I'm told that after the games, it will become apartments, offices, commercial space, and a parking lot. The building contains 237,000 square feet on two levels. CBS has seven hundred, or perhaps a thousand people here, depending on the source of your information. It is the biggest network contingent I've ever been part of.)

I am bewildered to be here. This did not fit my image of a retirement activity. Walking away from the studio with my family a year ago tonight, I did not envision myself in the French Alps a year later. I cannot think of a better symbol of retirement's surprises. Retirement is like the rest of life—fastball, curve, change-up.

I have written at Super Bowls and World Series and World Championship fights, but I had to retire to write about the Olympics.

I reread my retirement journal before I left New York. I am surprised to find how busy I have been this year, doing next to nothing. I do not know how I ever found time to work for a living. I am doing full time what I used to do for recreation when I worked, and I go to bed tired every night. I never found time, this first year, to do all that I wanted to do. I do not recall ever asking myself what to do or taking any action simply to fill time. So far, the reputed great monsters of retirement—angst, despair, boredom, aimlessness—are phantoms.

The reader will have noticed how much time I spend writing or thinking about writing or thinking about books, plays, movies, music. That is the sort of fellow I am. If I were a typical retired American, I probably would talk about other activities, but I suspect there is no more a typical retired person than there is a typical retirement year.

This year became atypical with the birth of Molly. The birth of a first grandchild defines a year. It is a once-in-a-lifetime event. The birth of the first grandchild is unique; the death of friends, alas, is not.

In going over my journal, I notice that I have managed to keep the activities of our children out of the narrative for the most part, just as I have managed to avoid identifying friends by name. I believe that private people have the right to privacy, even if they are the children or friends of a writer.

Betty, of course, cannot escape these pages. I cannot write about my retirement days and nights without writing of Betty. I cannot imagine what retirement would be without her, except lesser and lonely. The added hours I have with her are the best part of retirement.

Contrary to myth, I think that is probably true of most couples in retirement: the best part is that retirement gives them more time to be together. There are many more happy couples than you might guess from what you read and hear. Divorce makes news; wedding anniversaries don't.

I think Betty and I have been lucky, but I don't think we are special. In the early days of our marriage, we noticed older couples on the sidewalks of New York, holding hands, or we saw them in the park, jabbering and laughing. We said that's what we should be when we grow up. We all see our destinies in anonymous others.

I'm anticipating spending the next three weeks writing about an international sports festival that will bring together a record number of competitors for the event from a record number of countries. I am excited by the prospect.

And yet I am also only waiting for Betty. I am waiting for her to come to me in the Alps two weeks from now, in the middle of February. In the midst of this glamor and clamor, I peer sightless at an Alp, thinking of my wife. She will hang out with me, then visit her friends in Switzerland, then return, then we'll go to Italy. If you want to see a face light up, say "Venice" to almost anyone who has ever been there.

It may be the sense of anticipation realized, a sense of joy eases my way in retirement. The winter games equal Betty's arrival equals revelry in Venice. Equals the Super Bowl, a dinner party, laughter, and lust. Retirement seems to confirm the child's instinct that happiness arrives unbidden and is founded in the physical senses.

(One steaming July, a day or two before I was to leave my family on the island and return to New York, we had a major rainstorm. After it stopped the children, who probably ranged in age from about four to ten, asked Betty if they could play in the mud puddles that had formed in the yard. She gave them her blessing. They dashed from the house and the air soon was fragmented by the sounds of splashing and joyous howls. I never saw the children have more fun. They were returned to some state of precivilization. When they were tired and satisfactorily filthy, head to toe, we sent them to the lake for a swim and to wash off the mud. However sophisticated humans become, however elevated our tastes, there is a level at which joy begins as a child in the mud.)

Retirement is not free from concern. Betty's most recent visit to the eye doctor brought her news that her uninjured eye now appears to be at some risk. She will bring with her a list of doctors to see in France or Italy if she needs one.

Retirement is not even free from irritations. I have been trying to learn yet another damned computer, this one called a NewsMaker. I will only be using the machine for the next three weeks. Computers are like cars. No two are quite alike. *Where is the horn on this model?*

The serendipitous turn that puts me in the Alps may convey a warning. Perhaps this first year of retirement has been so happy because I was enchanted by the novelty of it. Retirement made everything new, even a walk around the block. Retirement may stale.

In the year I have been retired, however, I have not met one person who retired—as opposed to "was retired"—who is not happy in this condition. I heard of two, just two, cases of men who are miserable in retirement, and I read that there are more, but I did not meet any such person.

The retired people I talked with do not talk of retirement. They talk of what they are doing. Most retired on comfortable pensions and with money saved and invested. One fellow retired twenty years ago on a pension that seemed inadequate, and he is a portrait of content. No retired people I spoke with talked of money.

The people I talked to do a variety of things in retirement, and the computer now seems to play a role in what many retired men do. They fool around with their computers, sometimes plugging into elaborate networks. I think serious writing about retirement activity in the future will have to discuss computers.

A change I hope for in my retirement future is the chance to do some volunteer work. When it comes, I will not be doing it to fill time, which seems to fill itself.

Meanwhile, I wait for Betty. There will be a full moon when we are together in the Alps. I am confident there will be stars in Venice, where Corvo capered and Aschenbach died, where Wagner, hearing the gondoliers, wrote *Tristan,* and where *Traviata* failed on opening night, where Browning, like Shakespeare's Norfolk, gave his body to that pleasant country's earth, where on such a night as this, in Belmont . . .

Then we have Molly and the children to return to, friends to see. We have tickets in March for what is supposed to be a splendid revival of *The Most Happy Fella.* It is not too soon to think about the island. We may pause on our drive there to visit college friends in Madison. We must plan our New York Night and our Bastille Day and in September we will make our first trip to the Oregon Shakespeare Festival. I should concentrate on my study of Italian. I have to start writing the novel. I have the title, the first line, the story. I think I may even know how it ends.

Retirement? Let the games begin.